OXFORD REVISION GU

GCSE

ENGLISH
for Edexcel

Pam Taylor

Chief Examiner, GCSE English

OXFORD

UNIVERSITY PRESS

OXFORD
UNIVERSITY PRESS

Great Clarendon Street, Oxford OX2 6DP

Oxford University Press is a department of the University of Oxford.
It furthers the University's objective of excellence in research, scholarship,
and education by publishing worldwide in

Oxford New York
Athens Auckland Bangkok Bogotá Buenos Aires Cape Town
Chennai Dar es Salaam Delhi Florence Hong Kong Istanbul Karachi
Kolkata Kuala Lumpur Madrid Melbourne Mexico City Mumbai Nairobi
Paris São Paulo Shanghai Singapore Taipei Tokyo Toronto Warsaw
with associated companies in Berlin Ibadan

Oxford is a registered trade mark of Oxford University Press
in the UK and in certain other countries

First published 1999
This edition first published 2001

British Library Cataloguing in Publication Data

Data available

ISBN 0 19 831493 0

This edition assembled by Zed, Oxford

Printed by Ebenezer Baylis and Son Ltd., Worcester

contents

general introduction

A way forward

How will this book support you in your aim of doing well in English? We hope you will find it:

- useful in preparing you for your Edexcel GCSE English examinations;
- a helpful aid to your reading of the selected texts from *Tracks 2*, explaining some of the difficult points.

Above all, it should be:

- an aid to develop your own thinking and responses;
- a stimulus for discussion;
- a clear system for your revision.

The first half of the book goes through each of the requirements for the two examination papers, with explanations, suggestions and questions. The second half gives you sample questions, answers and commentaries.

> *Remember*, *the sooner you organise your thoughts and ideas, the easier you will find the preparation for all parts of the examination!*
>
> *This book aims to give you* **CONFIDENCE**.
>
> *You know you can succeed.*

ideas and approaches

Using your book

Here are a few ideas on how you might use this book.

Know your texts

It is very important to make sure that you have a really good grasp of the selected poems and non-fiction passages from *Tracks 2*. Every year, examiners read GCSE scripts where the candidates write in a way which shows that they do not understand, or have not prepared carefully, the texts which are set. Use the sections from this book to strengthen your knowledge of the texts.

Know your technical terms

As do all other subjects, English has a number of technical terms which you may need to use. It is important that you can use the correct term and that you can spell it. (Please refer to the useful glossaries on pages 39, 56 and 81.)

Know the types of writing required

These are:
- inform, explain, describe (see page 50);
- analyse, review, comment (see page 71–72);
- argue, persuade, instruct (see page 72–73).

Explore how to improve the structure and organisation of your answers. If you look closely at the model answers on pages 35–8, 52–5 and 75–80 and the examples of answers at different grades (pages 82–96) this will help you to write detailed, successful responses.

Presenting your work effectively

How you set out your own writing is important for various reasons. Get into the habit of producing writing that is:
- neat, regular and clear;
- spelt accurately;
- correctly punctuated;
- set out in clear paragraphs;
- laid out and presented well.

Apart from being good in themselves, such qualities in your writing will bring many benefits and advantages, both in the examination and afterwards.
- Examiners will form a positive impression of your work.
- They will not be slowed down or confused, as they will if the writing is hard to read and not written in proper sentences.
- How you write as well as what you write will be taken into account when your work is marked.
- Good writing is useful for applications for jobs or college courses.
- Many jobs need people who can write clearly, accurately and precisely.

Knowing your own strengths and weaknesses

It is an excellent idea to keep a checklist of your most common errors in spelling, punctuation and grammar.

- ○ When you receive a piece of work back from your teacher, read it through and make sure you understand any comments or corrections.
- ○ Keep a sheet of file paper at the front or back of your work file and write down on it the correct spelling of words you have misspelt.
- ○ Refer to this before handing in your work, to make sure you have not made the same mistakes.
- ○ Take some time to learn the correct spelling of all words on this list and check any points on punctuation and grammar you have noted.

Approach during your English course

Pay attention!

- ○ Listen to what teachers say.
- ○ Concentrate during class or group discussion.
- ○ Make certain you know what you have to do in class.
- ○ Be sure you understand what the homework is.
- ○ Check what your coursework assignments are.

Take part!

- ○ Ask questions in class.
- ○ Answer questions in class.
- ○ Contribute to discussion.
- ○ Be fully involved in group work.

(Your grade could depend on it!)

Make notes!

- ○ Keep clear records.
- ○ Write down key points from:
  - teachers
  - books you read
  - class work
  - articles or worksheets.
- ○ Annotate *Tracks 2* carefully (with your own interpretations).
- ○ Add points missed onto the end of your homework or practice questions when they are returned to you.

Keep up!

- ○ Hand work in on time.
- ○ Keep files or exercise books up to date.
- ○ Make sure homework does not get behind.
- ○ Do not leave work unfinished. (It is always difficult to remember what has been missed unless you amend it at the time.)
- ○ Check off completed work in your records.

Seek help!
○ Ask teachers to explain if you are unsure.
○ Discuss with friends.
○ Look things up by using:
  dictionaries
  encyclopædias
  the Internet.

Be organised!
○ Have clear systems.
○ Present work clearly.
○ Set yourself targets.
○ Stick to deadlines.
○ Keep your files neat and your notes together.
○ Organise yourself as you go through the course, as this is much better than trying to catch up at the last moment.

Approach to revision

Revising for examinations is a subject written about in many books, and these offer different suggestions and advice. What is certain is that not everything works for everyone. Each person has particular ways of revising and habits of working. Look at all the advice and try out the different suggestions. Decide clearly what are the **knowledge**, **skills** and **techniques** which you need to **acquire**, **develop**, **consolidate** or **revisit**.

What has to be done?
There are several steps.
○ Define the task.
○ Split it into its different parts or stages.
○ Identify your strengths and weaknesses.

Planning a schedule
○ Draw up a table to show the days and weeks before the examination.
○ Decide how much time to give to the subject in each week or day.
○ Work out a timetable with reasonable blocks of time.
○ Think about the need for variety and breaks.
○ Make sure your schedule is building towards a 'peak' at the right time.

How to improve
○ Test yourself.
○ Test a friend.
○ Practise examination questions.
○ Write to time limits, based on those in the actual examination.
○ Check your understanding of all texts, looking at words, meaning, plot and character.
○ Revise technical terms, using a **glossary**.
○ Be sure you can apply these properly, spell them properly, give examples, and explain how and why they are used.

Aids to learning

Write short, clear notes. Use such aids as:

- postcards
- diagrams
- flowcharts
- mnemonics (aids to memory, such as rhymes)
- computer programs
- audio tapes.

Other people

Do not try to go it alone. Ask others to check your progress, including:

- teachers
- parents, aunts or uncles
- elder or younger brothers/sisters
- classmates/friends.

Approach to exams

The whole of this book is designed to help you to approach the GCSE examinations in English with as much confidence as possible. Everyone knows that grades in the GCSE are regarded as being of great importance by many people. Particular courses of study, and very many forms of employment, require particular grades. This is especially true of English and Mathematics, which are basic requirements for all sorts of future occupations.

The importance of GCSE grades can create a sense of pressure. If managed properly, this can help your approach considerably, but if you're not careful it may also lead to too much worry and damage your performance.

Good preparation

Good preparation is one of the main elements affecting how people perform in examinations. This includes both attitude of mind and physical preparation.

1 Attitude of mind:
  - Be positive.
  - Be ready.
  - Be calm.

2 Physical preparation:
  - Be fit.
  - Be alert.
  - Be awake.

There are also specific things you need to do once in the examination room.

Come well-equipped

- Bring pens, pencils, rubbers, rulers and your copy of *Tracks 2*.
- Arrive in plenty of time.

Prepare and plan

- Take 5 to 10 minutes to check instructions and read the paper carefully.
- Decide how much time you need to allocate to each question. (You should aim to give about the same amount to each question, leaving five to ten minutes for checking through at the end.) Each English paper lasts two hours. An example of how to plan your time is shown below.

Reading the question paper	Question 1	Question 2	Question 3	Final Checking
5 mins	Planning – 5 mins Writing – 30 mins	Planning – 5 mins Writing – 30 mins	Planning – 5 mins Writing – 30 mins	10 mins
120 minutes (2 hours)				

- Write a brief plan for each answer (approximately 5 minutes).
- Look at any **key words** in the question, such as **compare**, **discuss** and **analyse**.
- Do not just copy out prepared notes, since they will not allow you to do the most important thing of all: **answer the question**.

Check your work

- Check that you are keeping to your planned timings.
- Keep thinking throughout about:
  - Relevance
  - Presentation
  - Accuracy
  - Varied vocabulary.

With your time at the end:
- Make sure you have answered all questions fully and appropriately.
- Correct any errors in **spelling** or **punctuation** (check, especially, that all sentences have full stops).
- Be certain everything can be read clearly.

Planning an answer

Answer the question!

Do not just write down everything you know! (This is the most common mistake made by examination candidates.)

Planning consists of the following elements:
- reading the question carefully and recognising what are the key words in it;
- deciding the main points you wish to make (what the question is looking for and how you intend to tackle it);
- selecting what you wish to include in the answer;
- giving your answer a structure: **introduction**, **main section(s)** and **conclusion**;
- choosing examples or quotations.

Thinking about the question

Identifying the **key words** in the question can help to show:

- what the question is looking for; and
- how you intend to tackle it.

Key words show what the examiner is expecting in setting this task. (There are often bullet points to help you.) For example:

- **Describe** asks you to show fully what you know about the content or character.
- **Explain** asks you to make clear to the examiner your understanding of the writing.
- **Discuss** invites you to weigh up both sides of an argument and come to your *own* conclusion.
- **Analyse** expects you to look closely and in detail at the writing and its effects.
- **Compare and contrast** asks for an examination of similarities and differences.
- **Give an appreciation of** seeks your personal response to the qualities of the writing.

Some of these words are covered in the sections from page 71 to page 73.

Key points

Write down quickly, in note form, your immediate thoughts about the subject. (You may find a diagram useful for this purpose.) Do not write full sentences here, or you will waste too much time.

The content of the answer

Try to include the following (the 'five vowels' mnemonic **A, E, I, O, U** may help you):

- **analysis**
- **ideas**
- **understanding.**
- **evidence**
- **opinions**

The examiner does want to know what you think: your own, personal **ideas** and **opinions**. But a series of unsupported statements starting with the words 'I think' is **not** enough, since the examiner also needs to know on what these ideas are based: the **analysis** of language and content, the **understanding** of the subject-matter, and the **evidence** on which your views are based.

Deciding the structure: introduction, main section(s) and conclusion

Introduction: A clear, brief introductory paragraph can make a very good initial impression, showing the examiner that you are thinking about the actual question.

Main Section(s): Decide how many paragraphs or sections you wish your answer to contain.

Conclusion: This may be quite a brief paragraph. It should sum up clearly and logically the argument that has gone before. Above all, it should show the examiner that you have **answered the question!**

Using quotations

When writing about English passages, whether books, poems, articles or extracts, one of the most important things is to use quotations. This is a skill which has to be practised. Over-use of quotations is as bad a mistake as not using any. You should use quotations especially for the following reasons:

- to illustrate or give an example (e.g. a simile or an instance of alliteration);
- to explain why you believe something (to support an opinion or argument or to prove a point).

Quotations should be short (one word to a line or two at the most), relevant and effective. Introduce quotations fluently into your sentence structure. Avoid saying 'He says'.

 *poetry*

Comparing and contrasting poems

On page 11, there was a reference to the fact that many questions ask you to 'compare and contrast' two poems. This section gives an example of two short poems, offered for comparison. These have been chosen so that you can think about how to set about such a comparison.

1 Read the two poems through at least twice. It is a very good idea to read them aloud once (or more). Most poems were written to be heard, and listening to their sound is an important part of understanding their meaning and effect. Check that you have grasped the basic ideas, and look up any words which you do not know in a dictionary.

When two poems are selected for this kind of comparison, there are usually some clear similarities – for example, of subject-matter – and also differences (such as the attitude of the poet towards this subject). This is true of the two poems on page 13.

It will help you to know that the two poems both come from the First World War (1914–1918). Rupert Brooke wrote 'The Soldier' right at the start of the war, before the trench warfare had commenced. Wilfred Owen wrote his 'Anthem for Doomed Youth' much later in the war (1917), after experiencing some of the worst of the battles, including the Somme. Think about the importance of this difference as you read the poems and respond to them. Underlining key words or phrases in different colours is one way to see which points you can link together, e.g. red for imagery, blue for attitudes to war.

2 Start with the obvious similarities:
  ○ Both are about war.
  ○ Both have 14 lines, one stanza of 8 and one of 6 (they are both sonnets).
  ○ Then look for other, perhaps less obvious subjects common to both, such as soldiers, death and burial.

3 Now think about the differences:
  ○ Brooke's is about himself, Owen's is about other people.
  ○ They show different attitudes to war and different attitudes to death.
  ○ Other differences:
      use of language
      rhyme and rhythm
      tone of voice.

4 In conclusion, think about your personal response:
  ○ Which poem do you prefer, and why?
  ○ Which makes the stronger impact, and how?

The Soldier

If I should die, think only this of me:
       That there's some corner of a foreign field
That is for ever England. There shall be
       In that rich earth a richer dust concealed;
A dust whom England bore, shaped, made aware,
       Gave, once, her flowers to love, her ways to roam,
A body of England's, breathing English air,
       Washed by the rivers, blest by suns of home.

And think, this heart, all evil shed away,
       A pulse in the eternal mind, no less
           Gives somewhere back the thoughts by England given;
Her sights and sounds; dreams happy as her day;
       And laughter, learnt of friends; and gentleness,
           In hearts at peace, under an English heaven.

Anthem for Doomed Youth

What passing-bells for these who die as cattle?
       Only the monstrous anger of the guns.
       Only the stuttering rifles' rapid rattle
Can patter out their hasty orisons.
No mockeries now for them; no prayers nor bells,
Nor any voice of mourning save the choirs, –
The shrill, demented choirs of wailing shells;
And bugles calling for them from sad shires.

What candles may be held to speed them all?
       Not in the hands of boys, but in their eyes
Shall shine the holy glimmers of goodbyes.
       The pallor of girls' brows shall be their pall;
Their flowers the tenderness of patient minds,
And each slow dusk a drawing-down of blinds.

U A Fanthorpe

Ursula (U A) Fanthorpe taught English and produced her first volume of poetry ('Side Effects') in 1978. Her first award for poetry was in 1980. She called herself 'a middle-aged drop-out'. After she left teaching, she worked in hospitals for many years. Her experiences with the young and the old have meant that she can write closely on their behaviour.

Half-past Two

checklist

Think about:

○ the boy

○ the teacher.

Underline:

○ all time words

○ all compound words

○ all sense ideas, e.g. sight, sound, smell

○ all feelings.

Think about:

○ what you like in the poem, and

○ why.

Write down

○ your ideas

○ and examples.

Half-past Two

Once upon a schooltime
He did Something Very Wrong
(I forget what it was).

And She said he'd done
Something Very Wrong, and must
Stay in the school-room till half-past two.

(Being cross, she'd forgotten
She hadn't taught him Time.
He was too scared of being wicked to remind her.)

He knew a lot of time: he knew
Gettinguptime, timeyouwereofftime,
Timetogohomenowtime, TVtime,

Timeformykisstime (that was Grantime).
All the important times he knew,
But not half-past two.

He knew the clockface, the little eyes
And two long legs for walking,
But he couldn't click its language,

So he waited, beyond onceupona,
Out of reach of all the timefors,
And knew he'd escaped for ever

Into the smell of old chrysanthemums on Her desk,
Into the silent noise his hangnail made,
Into the air outside the window, into ever.

And then, *My goodness*, she said,
Scuttling in, *I forgot all about you.*
Run along or you'll be late.

So she slotted him back into schooltime,
And he got home in time for teatime,
Nexttime, notimeforthatnowtime,

But he never forgot how once by not knowing time,
He escaped into the lockless land of ever,
Where time hides tick-less waiting to be born.

Thinking about 'Half-past Two'

The child

A schoolboy is the central character in the poem. Think about this boy.
- What age do you think he is?
- How does he feel, at various stages in the poem?
- What do we find out about the impression this event had on him?

The teacher
- How does she treat the boy?
- What do we find out about her?

The poem's effects
- You will see a large number of **compound words** in this poem - words made up of more than one word. Think carefully about these. Why does the poet use them?

Notice that these are all connected with **time**, which is a main theme in the poem – the title shows this.

- How many lines end with a 'time' word. Why is this important?

- The poet uses CAPITAL LETTERS in the words Something Very Wrong, which are repeated.
  What is the effect of this?
  What does this suggest about the boy and his thoughts?

- What does the poem tell us about:
  How time affects the boy's daily life;
  What he thinks and feels about time?

- Think about the world into which the boy escapes: 'the lockless land of ever'.
  How does he feel about this timeless world?

You may find it useful to consider some children's books in which children escape from the everyday world into an imaginary world, out of normal time, such as 'The Lion, The Witch and the Wardrobe' and the other books in the 'Chronicles of Narnia' series, 'Alice's Adventures in Wonderland' and 'Through the Looking Glass'. Do the children find such experiences frightening, magical, exciting? Are they pleased or disappointed to return to everyday 'reality'?

Reports

Has made a sound beginning
Strikes the right note:
Encouraging, but dull.
Don't give them anything
To take hold of.
Even pronouns are dangerous.

The good have no history.
So don't bother. *Satisfactory*
Should satisfy them.

Fair and *Quite good*.
Multi-purpose terms.
By meaning nothing.
Apply to all.
Feel free to deploy them.

Be on your guard:
Unmanageable oaf cuts both ways.
Finds the subject difficult,
Acquitting you, converts
Oaf into idiot, usher to master.

Parent, child, head.
Unholy trinity, will read
Your scripture backwards.
Set them no riddles, just
Echo the common-room cliché:
Must make more effort.

Remember your high calling:
School is the world.
Born at *Sound beginning*.
We move from *Satisfactory*
To *Fair*, then *Find*
The subject difficult.
Learning at last we
Could have done better.

Stone only, final instructor,
Modulates from the indicative
With *Rest in peace.*

Commentary

Here we imagine the teacher sitting down to start writing reports, and thinking what comment to write and how it will be taken.

The teacher's approach is very cautious, worried that whatever is written might lead to problems of some kind. The teacher might show a lack of knowledge of the pupil, by using 'he' rather than 'she'.

The good pupils haven't been difficult, so they won't be difficult in the future: it doesn't matter what you write about them.

Terms like this are inoffensive, and can be used for any pupil. The teacher will opt for the easy life by avoiding saying anything significant or constructive.

It's the difficult ones that are the problem. You don't want to suggest that you can't manage them. If you show that the problem is in the pupils, it leaves you firmly in control.

You have to be careful, because there are three separate readers, all of whom you have to satisfy. Keep it simple, since otherwise someone will read hidden meaning into it, treating it like a sacred text.

The teacher's reflections move on, seeing progress through school (or rather lack of it), as a 'metaphor' for life. It is a distinctly pessimistic view.

On death, the teacher's own report will be written on a gravestone: a release from all the trials (of teaching?).

checklist

○ Why are italics used?

○ What religious terms are used?

○ Why repeat some report comments?

○ Why are there so many commands?

glossary

Pronoun – a word which stands in place of a noun (for example, 'he' for 'the man')

Acquitting – setting free (from possible blame)

Trinity – a group of three persons (normally religious)

Common-room cliché – a boring phrase used in the staffroom

Modulates – changes (often in music)

Indicative – a grammatical term: the 'mood' used for making a statement, compared here with the 'imperative', used to give orders.

The teacher's four rules for writing reports:

- Don't give them anything to take hold of
- Don't bother
- Be on your guard
- Set them no riddles

Are these good rules?

What follows is an imaginary report. This is not a real pupil, and the comments are made-up; there is no significance in the subjects chosen. The comments are there to encourage you to think about what are the most helpful and unhelpful kinds of comments to receive, and what are the purposes of school reports.

Name _____   Form _____

Term _____   Absences _____

ENGLISH	She is an enthusiastic pupil, always willing to contribute her ideas.
HISTORY	Satisfactory.
GEOGRAPHY	Her attitude is so negative that I feel like giving up.
FRENCH	Although she finds some difficulties, she makes a real effort.
MATHEMATICS	A model pupil. Excellent!
DESIGN AND TECHNOLOGY	She behaves so badly that I don't know what to do with her.
SCIENCE	Disappointing.
PHYSICAL EDUCATION	Hard-working and committed, she always gives her very best.

It will not be difficult to say which of the comments a pupil would rather receive.

- But which, if any, are helpful?
- What would each member of the 'trinity' make of the comments:
  - parent
  - child
  - head?

Think about the reasons for writing reports:

- Telling the parent how the child is doing.
- Telling the child what to do to improve.
- Telling the head how pupils in the class are doing.
- Issuing praise, encouragement, warning.

Think about the meaning of the poem. It is called 'Reports', but is that the only subject? What do we learn about the teacher and about his or her view of

- life
- children
- teaching
- writing reports?

Is the teacher:

- committed to the pupils
- idealistic
- encouraging
- cynical
- disillusioned
- depressed
- afraid (if so, of what?)?

Dear Mr Lee

This poem takes the form of a letter to the writer, Laurie Lee. His most famous work is the autobiographical *Cider with Rosie*, written about his childhood in simple surroundings in the beautiful countryside of the Cotswold Hills in England. The poem also refers to another book by Laurie Lee, *As I Walked Out One Midsummer Morning*. This book describes the time when Laurie Lee left home and travelled to Spain.

Keep your copy of *Tracks 2* open at page 22 ('Dear Mr Lee') as you look at the following references:

Line 1   **Mr Smart** – the English teacher of the class in which one of the pupils is the imaginary writer of the letter.

Line 12   **T Hughes** – the poet, the late Ted Hughes (Poet Laureate)
                  P Larkin – the poet Philip Larkin
                  Both of these twentieth-century poets have written poems which are often studied for examinations.

Lines 22–24   In *Cider with Rosie*, Laurie Lee writes warmly and vividly about his mother.

Lines 26–27   Notice the change to *italics*.

Lines 34–35   **Terse:** brief, concise
                  Cogent: convincing

Line 36   Study closely the references to **poverty.**

Lines 38–40   The reference is to *As I Walked Out One Midsummer Morning*.

Line 49   *Cider* – *Cider with Rosie*.

- Have you underlined or ringed interesting examples of language and thought about how you could use them?

Character
What do we learn about the 'writer' of the letter's:
- likes and dislikes?
- attitudes to examinations?
- experience of learning English?
- relationship with Mr Smart – what kind of teacher is he?

Style and tone

Look at the length, structure and punctuation of the sentences in the poem.
What use, in particular, is made of:

- brackets ( )
- rhetorical questions
- the postscript (PS)?

As the poem is in the form of a letter, the 'writer' addresses Laurie Lee directly.

- How does this help to build up your sense of the relationship between the 'writer' and Laurie Lee?
- Does the poem seem to you to be serious or humorous? Find examples which show the tone.

Fanthorpe's intentions

- Why does the poet use contrasting language (**formal** and **informal**) at different times?
- What does she want us to feel about literature, examinations and writers?

Your response

How do you react to:

- the themes of the poems?
- the writer of the letter?
- the appeal of Laurie Lee?

> *Plan your ideas. Make sure you choose relevant examples.*

You Will Be Hearing From Us Shortly

As in the poem 'Dear Mr Lee' (see pages 18–19), the reader hears only one side of a communication. (We never learn what Laurie Lee thought of the letter.) This poem is a **dramatic monologue**, which presents only the words of the **interviewer**. The person who is really the 'subject' of the poem (the 'you' in the title, who is the '**interviewee**') never appears directly. We have to try to work out what he or she is like and what he or she is feeling.

- Study carefully what the 'interviewer' says and the way in which the words come across to you, by thinking about the questions below.

The interviewer's language

The interviewer's tone of voice is conveyed in a number of ways.

- The succession of questions. Pick out from this list the words which you feel best describe the tone of the questions:

reassuring	hostile	sympathetic	friendly
superior	bored	condescending	timid
aggressive	interested	snobbish	pompous
patronising	sarcastic	humble	helpful
intolerant	flexible	dismissive	thoughtful

Find examples which show the qualities which you have selected.
- The brief comments on the interviewee's imagined answers.
- The choice of very formal language.
- The comments on the information supplied on the application form.

The interviewee's feelings

What do you believe the interviewee's answers might have been? How do you feel that the interviewee would have felt:
- at the start of the poem?
- as it progressed?
- by the end?
- In writing this poem, what did Fanthorpe want us to feel?

A RECENT PARALLEL?

Recently, the newspapers carried a story of a lecturer who was criticised strongly for the way he spoke to a prospective student. It was claimed that he made remarks about the student's home background, suggesting that this could not have permitted a proper education.

- *Can you see any similarities?*

You Will Be Hearing From Us Shortly

You feel adequate to the demands of this position?
What qualities do you feel you
Personally have to offer?

                                                Ah

Let us consider your application form.
Your qualifications, though impressive are
Not, we must admit, precisely what
We had in mind. Would you care
To defend their relevance?

                                               Indeed

Now your age. Perhaps you feel able
To make your own comment about that,
Too? We are conscious ourselves
Of the need for a candidate with precisely
The right degree of immaturity.

                                        So glad we agree

And now a delicate matter: your looks.
You do appreciate this work involves
Contact with the actual public? Might they,
Perhaps, find your appearance
Disturbing?

                                            Quite so

And your accent. That is the way
You have always spoken, is it? What
Of your education? Were
You educated? We mean, of course,
Where were you educated?
And how
Much of a handicap is that to you,
Would you say?

                              Married, children,
We see. The usual dubious
Desire to perpetuate what had better
Not have happened at all. We do not
Ask what domestic disasters shimmer
Behind that vaguely unsuitable address.

And you were born – ?

                                          Yes. Pity.

So glad we agree.

The interviewee

- Do you think this person is more likely to be a man or a woman?
- Does it matter?
- What do we learn about the person's looks and background?
- How much does the poem enable us to find out about the person who is being interviewed?
- What can we work out from the limited information given and from the **tone** of the questions?

The interviewer

- What do we learn about the interviewer? Again, the poem does not tell us the sex (What do you think? Man? Woman? Impossible to tell?), age or looks, but certainly it presents much information about the person's attitudes.
- How does your understanding of the interviewer's attitudes help you to get a grasp of the **themes** and **purposes** of this poem?

Not My Best Side

Keep your copy of *Tracks 2* open at pages 25–26 ('Not My Best Side') as you look at the following references:

Section I *(lines 1–19)* THE DRAGON

Line 11	*ostentatiously* – very obviously	
Line 14	*inedible* – uneatable	
Line 15	*literally* – really, actually (not used as a figure of speech)	

Section 2 *(lines 20–38)* THE VIRGIN

Line 32	*hardware* – a computing term, used here for St George's armour

Section 3 *(lines 39–57)* SAINT GEORGE

Line 39	*reclamation* – rescue, recovery
Line 41	*automatic transmission* – a car term – no manual gearbox
Line 42–43	*built-in obsolescence* – not meant to last long, like modern machines
Line 44	*prototype* – original design

This poem is an example of how a poet can be inspired by a picture. The painting on page 26 of *Tracks 2* is in the National Gallery in London, and U A Fanthorpe wrote that she 'thought it might be interesting to find voices for characters who are conventionally good, bad or helpless'.

The poem is written in three distinct sections, each consisting of 19 lines. The three sections represent the three different **viewpoints** and **voices** in the poem, and each is a **dramatic monologue**: the poet takes on the voice, in turn, of the Dragon, the Virgin and Saint George.

In legend, of course, these characters are **stereotypes** of basic ideas:

○ **The Dragon** stands for evil: a killer and destroyer of purity.
○ **The Virgin** is the innocent victim, rescued by the hero.
○ **Saint George**, England's national saint, is the original 'knight in shining armour', rescuing the damsel and killing off evil.

The poem therefore raises a number of questions about how we look at pictures, but also how we look at ideas and people.

- Do those who are stereotyped turn out as we expect?
- Are people's emotions and motives more complex than a simple picture would suggest?
- What contrast is there between the 'conventional' characters and the modern qualities which the three dramatic monologues reveal?

Based on the poem, analyse the personality of each of the three characters. Think about these questions:

- What is unexpected about each?
- Which do you find sympathetic (if any) and why?
- Does the title apply to only one character, or to all three, do you think? Why do you feel this?
- Are all the dramatic monologues equally good, do you think? How well does each character come to life?
- How does Fanthorpe use humour to make the characters more vivid? Look at such examples as: 'diplomas in Dragon Management and Virgin Reclamation'.

Study the picture again. In what ways do you look at it differently now from your first impressions?

A revision guide to the use of quotations in poetry answers, using the poems of U A Fanthorpe as an example

Here are **ten pointers** which should help to ensure success in your answers:

1 Include well-chosen quotations, making sure that they support your critical points.

2 Remember the sequence: **critical point: illustration: comment.**

3 Keep quotations brief – that is – restrict yourself to the **key**, **relevant** words or phrases.

4 It is unlikely that a quotation which is more than **two lines long** will be entirely relevant.

5 Mark all quotations clearly by placing them inside **quotation marks**.

6 Wherever possible, include the quotation within your own sentence structure.

7 Do not list quotations: use them.

8 Introductory comments which identify the poet's technique will enable you to make the most of your examples, e.g.: 'the poet uses repetition skilfully in the words....'

9 Do not just give the names or number of technical features or devices. Never simply say, for example: 'There are four similes in this poem....'

10 Keep to the positive – do not refer to what is not there, for example: 'There is no alliteration in this poem'. There is no rule which states that all poems must include certain devices.

Using quotations – some examples

The examples which follow offer some ways of working quotations into your sentences, using poems by U A Fanthorpe as an illustration.

Sound: *(Half-past Two)* *Fanthorpe stresses the mechanical, hard sound of the clock in the words 'clockface' and 'click'.*

Imagery: *(Not My Best Side)* *In describing the horse of St George, Fanthorpe talks about its 'automatic transmission' and 'built-in obsolescence', which are images taken from the world of cars and the machinery of modern life.*

Repetition: *(Half-past Two)* *In the eighth stanza, Fanthorpe starts each line with the words 'into the'. This repetition seems to emphasise the escapist journey which the child is making away from the reality of his situation.*

Tone: *(Not My Best Side)* *The tone adopted by the supposed maiden is very far from that which you would expect from the legend, since her use of words like 'you could see all his equipment' shows she is a very 'modern' girl, and she uses innuendo to show the reader what she is after.*

Attitude: *(Not My Best Side)* *The poet makes St George demonstrate rather sexist and arrogant attitudes in the way he speaks to the girl, with phrases such as 'So why be difficult?' and 'You're in my way'.*

Vernon Scannell

Vernon Scannell was born in 1922. During the Second World War he served in the military. He continued after the war to have a life of adventure, since for a short time he became a professional boxer. It is probable that he is the only successful poet ever to have combined these two professions! He became interested in poetry by chance, while flicking through the pages of a book in a second-hand bookshop. He decided that very moment that what he wanted was to become a poet. As well as writing, he has done much broadcasting and lecturing.

Hide and Seek

Call out. Call loud: 'I'm ready! Come and find me!'
The sacks in the toolshed smell like the seaside. ◄—— Simile
They'll never find you in this salty dark.
But be careful that your feet aren't sticking out.
Wiser not to risk another shout.
The floor is cold. They'll probably be searching
The bushes near the swing. Whatever happens
You mustn't sneeze when they come prowling in.
And here they are, whispering at the door;
You've never heard them sound so hushed before.
Don't breathe. Don't move. Stay dumb. Hide in your blindness. ◄—— Metaphor
They're moving closer, someone stumbles, mutters;
Their words and laughter scuffle, and they're gone.
But don't come out just yet: they'll try the lane
And then the greenhouse and back here again.
They must be thinking that you're very clever,
Getting more puzzled as they search all over.
It seems a long time since they went away.
Your legs are stiff, the cold bites through your coat;
The dark damp smell of sand moves in your throat.
It's time to let them know that you're the winner.
Push off the sacks. Uncurl and stretch. That's better!
Out of the shed and call to them: 'I've won!
Here I am! Come and own up I've caught you!'
The darkening garden watches. Nothing stirs. }—— Personification
The bushes hold their breath; the sun is gone.
Yes, here you are. But where are they who sought you?

checklist

- Colour code words which appeal to the different **senses**

- Note use of **direct speech**

- Look at **similes, metaphors** and **personification** and think about why they are used

- Note the **rhetorical question** at the end and its purpose

- Note use of short sentences and commands

Hide-and-seek is one of the best-known of all childhood games, at least for those who grew up as children in this country, with its familiar cry of 'Coming, ready or not' and the counting down to the start of the search:

- Did you play it?
- If so, what do you most remember about it – the hiding or the seeking? Why?
- Are your memories of it happy, 'scary', or what?

What did the child feel?

Look at the different feelings which the child who was hiding had during the poem. You may find it useful to divide the poem into sections, in order to see how these feelings change at different points, and list the feelings in each section.

Lines 1–4   The child hides.
Lines 5–8   The child waits.
Lines 9–13   The other children arrive and then leave.
Lines 14–17   The child decides to wait a little longer.
Lines 18–21   The child decides the wait has been long enough.
Lines 22–24   The child emerges from the hiding-place.
Lines 25–27   The child discovers that the other children have all gone.

Turn to the model answer on pages 35–36 of this book. Compare the points made there about the child's feelings with your own analysis.

Use of the senses

This is a poem in which all five senses are used to help the reader imagine the experiences of the young child:

Hearing   Line 1: the sound of the children's voices is present right from the first word.
Smell   Line 2: the smell of the seaside.
Taste   Line 3: the taste of salt.
Sight   Line 3: it is dark; the child cannot see or be seen.
Touch   Line 4: his feet must be touching the sacks, wrapped inside them.

So within the first four lines, all five senses have been involved.

Such references occur throughout the poem, too.

You could draw up five columns and list the references under them:

Hearing	Smell	Taste	Sight	Touch

What does this poem tell us

- About the child
- About children
- About human nature?
- About childhood games
- About childhood

Poets and childhood

In *Tracks 2* you will read several poems which deal with particular stages of childhood. All of them deal with events which were, in some way, difficult or unhappy for the child.

- Why do poets seem to concentrate on the 'down' side of being a child?
- Do we tend to remember things which were difficult or unhappy? If so, why?
- Do you remember moments which were 'key points' ('crossroads' events) in your own life?
- Are these events from which you learnt something useful or important?
- What do you think the child may have learnt from this game of 'hide-and-seek'?

Hugo Williams

Hugo Williams was born in Windsor, Berkshire, in 1942 to a well-known English theatrical family. He worked on the *London Magazine* from 1961 to 1970. Since that time, he has worked as a journalist, poet and travel writer. He has published many volumes of poetry and his most recent collection, *Billy's Rain*, won him the TS Eliot Prize in 2000. His poems are in a very direct style, which makes them easy for readers to respond to. This applies strongly in the case of 'Leaving School'.

Leaving School

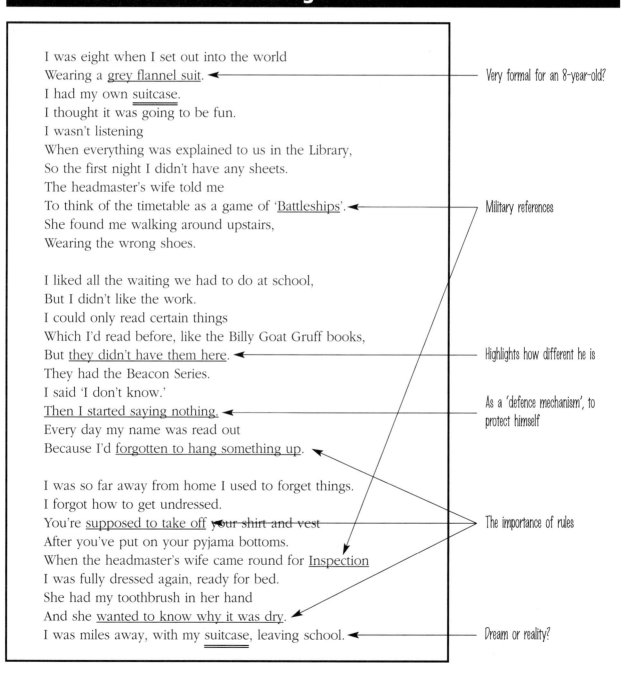

I was eight when I set out into the world
Wearing a grey flannel suit. ◄——————— Very formal for an 8-year-old?
I had my own suitcase.
I thought it was going to be fun.
I wasn't listening
When everything was explained to us in the Library,
So the first night I didn't have any sheets.
The headmaster's wife told me
To think of the timetable as a game of 'Battleships'. ◄——————— Military references
She found me walking around upstairs,
Wearing the wrong shoes.

I liked all the waiting we had to do at school,
But I didn't like the work.
I could only read certain things
Which I'd read before, like the Billy Goat Gruff books,
But they didn't have them here. ◄——————— Highlights how different he is
They had the Beacon Series.
I said 'I don't know.'
Then I started saying nothing. ◄——————— As a 'defence mechanism', to protect himself
Every day my name was read out
Because I'd forgotten to hang something up.

I was so far away from home I used to forget things.
I forgot how to get undressed.
You're supposed to take off your shirt and vest
After you've put on your pyjama bottoms.
When the headmaster's wife came round for Inspection
I was fully dressed again, ready for bed. ◄——————— The importance of rules
She had my toothbrush in her hand
And she wanted to know why it was dry.
I was miles away, with my suitcase, leaving school. ◄——————— Dream or reality?

Look at:
- What we learn about the school
  - the people
  - the rules
  - the routines
  - the lessons

- What we learn about the boy
  - his nature
  - his feelings

- What we learn about his difficulties
  - not knowing what to do
  - getting things wrong
  - being confused
  - not understanding
  - feeling different
  - being isolated

- What happens at the end
  - the headmaster's wife's actions
  - the last line

Choose words which you think sum up the boy's feelings, at the different stages of the poem, from the following list, or add your own:

relief	disappointment	sorrow	excitement
escapism	rebellion	frustration	happiness
expectation	confusion	apprehension	anxiety
insecurity	confidence	panic	ignorance

Where you have chosen a word, place it next to words in the poem which show these feelings.

Think about:
- The significance of the title
- The importance in the poem of the boy's suitcase
- The part played in the poem by his clothes
- The verbs he uses to describe his feelings or actions (eg 'liked', 'forgot')
- The importance of the change in mood at the end

Exploring the language:
- The diction and register (e.g. is it simple and childlike or adult and complex?)
- The tone of voice (e.g. is it matter-of-fact or emotional?)
- The sentence structure, length and style (e.g. short and straightforward or long and difficult?)

Wole Soyinka

Wole Soyinka is a playwright, poet, novelist and lecturer. He was born in Nigeria and went to university there before studying at Leeds University in England. He then returned to Nigeria, but was arrested and imprisoned by the government during the civil war and was in prison for two years. His stay in prison inspired him to write poetry and plays. He often wrote about the need for individual freedom.

Telephone Conversation

The price seemed reasonable, location
Indifferent. The landlady swore she lived
Off premises. Nothing remained
But self-confession. 'Madam,' I warned.
'I hate a wasted journey – I am African.'
Silence. Silenced transmission of
Pressurised good-breeding. Voice, when it came,
Lipstick coated, long **gold**-rolled
Cigarette holder pipped. Caught I was, foully.
'HOW **DARK**?'… I had not misheard…'ARE YOU **LIGHT**
OR **VERY DARK**?' Button B. Button A. Stench
Of rancid breath of public hide-and-speak.
Red booth. **Red** pillar-box. **Red** double-tiered
Omnibus squelching **tar**. It *was* real! Shamed
By ill-mannered silence, surrender
Pushed dumbfounded to beg simplification.
Considerate she was, varying the emphasis –
ARE YOU **DARK**? OR **VERY LIGHT**? Revelation came.
'You mean – like **plain or milk chocolate**?'
Her assent was clinical, crushing in its light
Impersonality. Rapidly, wave-length adjusted
I choose. 'West African **sepia**' – and as an afterthought,
'Down in my passport.' Silence of **spectroscopic**
Flight of fancy, till truthfulness clanged her accent
Hard on the mouthpiece. 'WHAT'S THAT?' conceding
'DON'T KNOW WHAT THAT IS.' 'Like **brunette**.'
'THAT'S **DARK**, ISN'T IT?' 'Not altogether.
Facially, I am **brunette**, but madam, you should see
The rest of me. Palm of my hand, soles of my feet,
Are a **peroxide blonde**. Friction, caused –
Foolishly, madam – by sitting down, has turned
My bottom **raven black** – One moment madam!' – sensing
Her receiver rearing on the thunderclap
About my ears – 'Madam,' I pleaded, 'wouldn't you rather
See for yourself?'

Why does he say 'warned'?

Repetition

Think about these descriptions of how she speaks

Old-fashioned telephones had two buttons to press

Coldness

checklist

○ Colour code the words of the two speakers

○ Think about the 'colour' words marked in bold here

glossary

rancid – smelling stale

sepia – dark brown

spectroscopic – breaking down colours, as if with a spectroscope

conceding – admitting

The landlady

friendly
unwelcoming
tolerant
sympathetic
negative
afraid
generous
hesitant
polite
shocked
inquisitive
interested
prejudiced
condescending
sensitive
racist

The narrator

desperate
flippant
friendly
open-minded
intelligent
witty
anti-racist
insulting
outraged
disbelieving
resentful
naive

The two characters

What can we learn about the two characters from the conversation and from the narrator's comments? Choose from the lists on the left those words which you think apply, and add others of your own choice.

Which parts of the poem give you most understanding of the characters: the telephone conversation itself or the narrator's comments?

Colour prejudice

The poem deals with the subject of racial prejudice, and in particular prejudice about the colour of someone's skin. At the time it was written, it was not illegal for the landlady to refuse to have a black man as a tenant. Since then, laws have been introduced to try to remove discrimination on the grounds of race, and human rights are protected more strongly now, although prejudice and discrimination certainly still exist. If a landlady today turned a black man away simply because he was black, she could be prosecuted.

Colour in the poem

The poem shows that the landlady really wanted to know just what colour the man on the other end of the line was, and so words to do with colour are very important. Colour words have been printed in bold on page 28.

- Why does the landlady seem so worried about exactly what shade of brown, or what degree of darkness, the man's skin colour is?
- Why does the man choose the words 'sepia' and then 'brunette' to describe his skin colour?
- Why does he then mention that parts of his body are different colours, blonde and black? Why is the colour 'red' introduced in the poem? Was the man 'seeing red' (that is, angry?) Did he imagine the landlady's red-coated lips spitting him out, like the bus squelching the black tyre?

Humour as a 'defence mechanism'

People sometimes use humour as a way of defending themselves when under attack.

- Pick out examples of the writer's use of humour.
- What do these show us about the man in the poem?
- Was it a good idea for him to try to be funny?

The language and ideas of the poem

- What other features do you notice in the writer's use of language?
- How do these contribute to the poem's effectiveness?
- What is the poet trying to convey in this poem?
- How, if at all, has this poem changed or influenced your views?

U A Fanthorpe

Old Man, Old Man

He lives in a world of small recalcitrant
Things in bottles, with tacky labels. He was always
A man who did-it-himself.

Now his hands shamble among clues
He left for himself when he saw better,
And small things distress: *I've lost the hammer.*

<u>Lifelong adjuster of environments,</u>
<u>Lord once of shed, garage and garden,</u>
Each with its proper complement of tackle.

<u>World authority</u> on twelve different
Sorts of glue, <u>connoisseur of nuts</u>
<u>And bolts,</u> not good with daughters

An outdoor man: he controlled his outdoor empire

But a dab hand with the Black and Decker,
Self-demoted in your nineties to washing-up
After supper, and missing crusted streaks

now he is largely confined to the house

No good with daughters:

Of food on plates: have you forgotten
The jokes you no longer tell, as you forget
If you've smoked your timetabled cigarette?

his wife had to take down their pictures

Now television has no power to arouse
Your surliness; your wife could replace on the walls
Those pictures of disinherited children.

but still wants to be out and about.

He can hardly see but he can be seen.

and the children were **disinherited** – cut out of his will, or inheritance.

And you wouldn't know. Now you ramble
In your talk around London districts, fretting
At how to find your way from Holborn to Soho.

He hates being helpless but can only get out with help.

And where is Drury Lane? <u>Old man, old man,</u>
So obdurate in your contracted world,
<u>Living in almost-dark,</u> *I can see you,*

Repetition (the words of the title)

You said to me, *but only as a cloud.*
When I left, you tried not to cry. I love
Your helplessness, you who hate being helpless.

Let me find your hammer. Let me
Walk with you to Drury Lane. I am only a cloud.

Only a cloud:
Why does she say this?
Is it because he is no good with people?
Is a cloud less of a threat?
It won't undermine his independence, perhaps, as a wife or daughter would?

glossary

Recalcitrant – awkward, not doing what you want

shamble – fumble, shuffle around

complement – the right amount

connoisseur – someone who knows all about something

fretting – worrying

obdurate – obstinate, difficult

contracted – grown smaller

Think about:

- The title
  - it suggests someone talking to an old man. This person could be talking in very different tones, feeling: pitying; sympathetic; angry; exasperated; frustrated; trying to make oneself heard or understood; telling him off.
  - The use of the repetition is the striking thing. If it just said 'Old Man', it would be very different.
  - The words 'Old man, old man' appear later in the poem, too (line 25). By this time we have learnt much more about the old man and the writer's (U A Fanthorpe's) thoughts about him.

- The writer's attitudes
  - After you have read the poem, what do you think Fanthorpe's feelings and attitudes towards the old man really are? Draw up two columns and write down the evidence you find in the poem about her feelings. Two suggestions are offered to start you thinking:

Feelings towards him	Feelings against him
I love your helplessness	Not good with daughters

From this list, what do we learn about the relationship between the narrator and the old man?

- The old man

  In the past
  - What he was good at:
    world authority on …. glue
    connoisseur of nuts
    a man who did-it-himself
    a dab hand with the Black and Decker
  - What he was not good at:
    not good with daughters
    television (it aroused his surliness)

  In the present
  - What he is like now:

his hands shamble	*he frets*
forgetful	*he is obdurate*
rambles in his talk	*he is helpless*
he can hardly see	*he is unhappy*

  In the future….
  'At the crossroads'?
  - Why do you think this poem is included in a section with this title?
  - Has the old man reached a 'crossroads' in his life? If so, what is it, and what are the possible roads that lie ahead?

Two pictures of old age

The next poem in the selection is also about old age, 'Warning'.
It presents a very different picture.
Which poem do you prefer and why?
Compare your response with that of others in the class.

Jenny Joseph

Jenny Joseph studied at Oxford University and later trained as a newspaper reporter. She has since done various jobs, including lecturing in English and being a pub landlady, and has published both prose and poetry, working with photographers, painters, musicians and actors. By far her best-known poem, both in Britain and America, is 'Warning'. It has won many awards and was voted best poem in the last fifty years in a BBC Television poll.

> **DISGRACEFUL VERSE TOPS POLL**
>
> *A lyrical homage to growing old disgracefully by the Gloucestershire poet Jenny Joseph is topping a poll to find the nation's favourite poem of the past half-century. Joseph, 64, is a winner of the Forward Prize and 'Warning' has been in a number of collections. Her first book of poems was published in 1960 and immediately won an award, as did her second collection and subsequent books. The Times Literary Supplement has described her best poems as revealing 'a world living in the clutches of disappointment and mortality, but open to the possibility of intense delight in minute but dazzling particulars of nature and in rare acts of human kindness'.*
>
> David Lister, *The Independant* newspaper, 10 October 1996

Warning

checklist

Note the use of pronouns, shown in **bold type**, here: what is the importance of the changes from the first person singular?

glossary

sobriety – being sober and serious

hoard – collect a store

NOTE CONTRAST BETWEEN RECKLESSNESS AND CONFORMITY

When **I** am an old woman **I shall** wear purple
With a red hat which doesn't go, and doesn't suit **me**.
And **I shall** spend **my** pension on brandy and summer gloves
And satin sandals, and say we've no money for butter.
I shall sit down on the pavement when **I'm** tired
And gobble up samples in shops and press alarm bells
And run **my** stick along the public railings
And make up for the sobriety of **my** youth.
I shall go out in my slippers in the rain
And pick the flowers in other people's gardens
And learn to spit.

You can wear terrible shirts and grow more fat
And eat three pounds of sausages at a go
Or only bread and pickle for a week
And hoard pens and pencils and beermats and things in boxes.

But now **we must** have clothes that keep **us** dry
And pay **our** rent and not swear in the street
And set a good example for the children.
We must have friends to dinner and read the papers.

But maybe **I ought** to practise a little now?
So people who know **me** are not too shocked and surprised
When suddenly **I** am old, and start to wear purple.

**THE FUTURE
(I shall)** wear…
spend…
say…
sit…
gobble…
run…
make up…
go out…
pick…
learn…

(You can) wear…
eat…

hoard…

**THE PRESENT
(We must)** have…
pay…
set…
read…

**PREPARING FOR THE FUTURE IN THE PRESENT
(I ought)** practise…
start…

A popular success

In an interview Jenny Joseph gave, she was asked to explain the popularity of her poem 'Warning'. She said that 'Warning' had many things that people liked.

> 'To begin with there are things and activities in it rather than general statements. There is colour, food, flowers, and gardens. There are children, shops, and money; above all there are clothes. (I knew that mentioning sausages sets the saliva flowing but had no idea that there were so many people who would take to their heart anything that is purple or has the word in it. I can't stand it. That, of course, is why it's in the poem.)'
>
> *The Lancet, November 1999*

Jenny Joseph mentions here that the poem contains references to many everyday things, and things which people like: colour, food, clothes, for example.

- How important are these in your response to the poem?
- How different a poem would it have been if the writer had chosen different colours and objects: 'blue and yellow', for example, rather than 'purple and red'; 'cabbages' instead of sausages'?
- What does this tell us about the importance in a poem of selecting exactly the right word?

The old woman

- What sort of character is the old woman imagined to be?
- How do you think you would react if you met an old woman acting like this?
- How do you think other people would react?
- Do you know anyone who is at all like this?

Time

This is a poem which deals mainly with the future. You can see from page 32 that most of the lines are looking forward to the future, and the poem starts and ends with the same idea (what is known as 'ring composition'). But there is also an important short section which focuses on the woman's life at present.

- What do we find out about the life that the woman is living at present?
- What is her attitude towards this life?
- How does this contribute to her thoughts about the future?
- How is she intending to prepare for this future life straightaway?
- In what ways does this suggest that she is at a crossroads in her life?
- To what extent is it fair to describe the woman as a 'rebel', and, if it is, what is she rebelling against?

Interpreting the poem

Look at the following quotations from the interview given by Jenny Joseph. Think how these might help you to interpret the poem.

> 'The use of the first person in a story makes it sound intimate. The listener/reader hears someone talking and includes him/herself in the scene.'
>
> 'When she uses the first plural she includes the husband further in her detailing of everyday present life, completing the family picture with the children and other people (third person plural).'
>
> 'She'll be there, all right, through as many days as it takes, solid as a rock, cooking dinner, chivvying, respectable, worrying, cheering them up.'
>
> 'People, perhaps remembering a growing-up somewhat weighted with disapproval by elders or leading a life onerous from pressure to succeed, have been grateful that someone was thumbing her nose at censoriousness, at disapproval, and winning.'
>
> 'Although there is irony... there is not the cruelty of satire or mockery – in fact, the poem is against mockery.'
>
> *The Lancet, November 1999*

'At the crossroads' poetry specimen questions: Question 1 (2F/4H)

The following are examples to help you to revise and plan your answers. They are intended to assist with preparation and revision for both tiers. For examinations from Summer 2002, the specified poet for these questions will be U A Fanthorpe.

U A Fanthorpe

Half-past Two
- Look at the references to time in this poem. How does time affect the pupil?
- How does the poem explore the ideas of 'knowing' and 'not knowing'? Refer closely to the poem.

Reports
- What does U A Fanthorpe suggest about the kinds of language often used in school reports?
- Does this seem to you to be an optimistic or pessimistic poem? Explain your answer by reference to the language used by U A Fanthorpe.

Dear Mr Lee
- What does the poem suggest about studying literature for an examination?
- Why does the 'writer' feel so differently about the work of Laurie Lee, compared with that of other authors? Support your answer with examples from the text.

You Will Be Hearing From Us Shortly
- What does this poem make you feel about the process of being interviewed?
- In what ways do the words of the interviewer undermine the person who is being interviewed?

Not My Best Side
- Study closely the second section (on the virgin). What kind of person does her language show her to be, and how might this be thought surprising?
- In what ways does the poem affect your view of the picture and the legend it deals with?

Old Man, Old Man
- How much sympathy do you feel the poem shows for the old man?
- What is the importance in this poem of the theme of 'do it yourself'?

Vernon Scannell

Hide and Seek
- How does Vernon Scannell's language convey the various feelings of the child playing 'hide-and-seek'? Refer closely to the text to support your answer.
- Compare the impression which Scannell creates of childhood in this poem with that given by Hugo Williams in 'Leaving School'.

Hugo Williams

Leaving School
- How do the child's feelings about school change over time?
- What impression does Hugo Williams give of life in a boarding school?

Wole Soyinka

Telephone Conversation
- What impression does this poem give (a) of the man speaking in the poem and (b) of the landlady?
- How does Wole Soyinka use colour in this poem to reinforce his theme?

Jenny Joseph

Warning
- In what ways does Jenny Joseph create humour by the descriptions and images she uses?
- What message is Jenny Joseph trying to convey about the theme of growing old?

Model answers for 'At the crossroads' poetry selection

On page 34, there are a number of questions on the poems set for Question 1 on both Paper 2F and Paper 4H. You may wish to use these in the following three ways:

1 Take five minutes to plan an answer, using the relevant poem from *Tracks 2*.
2 Choose any one question and make a list of the quotations and references you would use in your answer; write notes on how you would comment on these.
3 Practise writing one or more questions to time, allowing yourself no more than 40 minutes for planning and writing.

Question 1

Remember the assessment objectives for this question: They are:
i) Main Assessment Objective: to develop and sustain interpretation of text
ii) Supporting Assessment Objectives:
  ○ to read with insight and engagement;
  ○ to make appropriate reference to the text.

A good answer will show
  ○ a personal response to the situations, characters and language;
  ○ the ability to select and use examples to support your views.

You should not just list a large number of technical features or facts in your answer. You should look closely at all **key words** in the question and in the poem before starting your answer.

Example 1: Dear Mr Lee (Fanthorpe)

  • **Why does the 'writer' feel so differently about the work of Laurie Lee, compared with that of other authors? Support your answer with examples from the text.**

Note the key words in the question: **feel**, **differently**, **Laurie Lee**, **other authors**, **examples.**
  ○ You need to consider the feelings of the letter-writer for Laurie Lee.
  ○ There should be a comparison with the writer's attitude to the other authors mentioned.
  ○ Ideas must be supported from what the poem says.

Model Answer

In the poem 'Dear Mr Lee', Fanthorpe quickly establishes the close rapport felt by the imagined writer of the letter with Laurie Lee, and observes that this is despite the fact that the book ('Cider with Rosie') is being studied as an examination text. A strong contrast is made between Lee's work and that of the other writers who have been introduced.

It is clear that this pupil 'used to hate English', and did not find it easy to respond to the so-called great writers such as Shakespeare, who is likened to a 'national disaster' — a phrase which recognises how much of a national figure Shakespeare is, but shows no appreciation of his writing. It seems that the writer of the letter finds it a chore to study him because his language and ideas are not easily accessible. The writer seems disdainful that Mr Smart has to 'explain why they're jokes' and even then nobody laughs.

It is not only Shakespeare but also T Hughes and P Larkin, other poets whose works have to be studied, that fail to interest the pupil. The difference in the writer's attitude is evident. Laurie Lee is addressed as 'Dear Mr Lee' or even 'Laurie', yet only initials are used for Larkin and Hughes. The pupil finds them distant and is detached from them. Lee, on the other hand, is a comfort and a companion through all difficult times. The tone is chatty and informal; his book is 'the one that made up for the others'.

'Cider with Rosie' is a book which the writer actually wishes to study, and even learns parts of it by heart, not because it is a set text but because it can cheer somebody up and can ease a cold: the pupil even takes the book to bed. The characters in 'Cider with Rosie' are ones who are real, especially Lee's mother, half-sisters and uncles. The situations are warm, friendly and humorous.

The language chosen to contrast other writers with Lee, and also to highlight the approach adopted by examinations, emphasises how strongly the writer of the letter feels. Examinations are, it seems, the enemy of enjoyment for this reader at least. The relationship built up with Laurie Lee is somehow destroyed if the writer has to analyse characters in a cold and unfeeling way: it seemed 'wrong' to reduce the character of Laurie's mother to a sketch under 'headings', or to think about the society in which he lived solely in terms of social welfare in a rural community'. The words used in examination questions such as 'seasons as perceived by an adolescent' are equally off-putting.

Finally, Fanthorpe allows the letter-writer to express with great clarity the nature of the response which Lee's writing has generated. This stems especially from Lee's ability to observe the world and people closely: 'to see everything bright and strange'. The writer can identify with Lee's view of the world, including even the material poverty of his upbringing, and still see everything in positive terms. 'Cider with Rosie', for this reader, was able to unlock an appreciation of literature which dull teaching, tedious examination questions and unsympathetic authors had failed to arouse.

Example 2: Hide and Seek (Scannell)

- **How does Vernon Scannell's language convey the various feelings of the child playing 'hide-and-seek'? Refer closely to the text to support your answer.**

Note the key words in the question: **language, feelings**.
- the question is about the **child hiding**, not the **other children.**
- you must support your views by **examples** from the poem.

Model Answer
This is not intended to be an 'ideal' answer, but to illustrate the approach looked for.

Vernon Scannell uses the perspective of a child to convey the feelings of a young child when playing hide-and-seek. This device works extremely effectively, enabling the reader to put him or herself closely into the mind of the young child.

The child who has been chosen in the game to hide (we assume it is a boy, but the sex is not stated) is very excited once the game starts. He wants those who are seeking him to have to work particularly hard to locate his hiding-place. We hear the excitement in his voice when he calls 'I'm ready! Come and find me!' The child believes that he will be able to escape detection because of his skill at hiding.

It is vitally important that he has the best possible place to hide. We see how important it is to him to have everything meticulously prepared: he thinks 'Be careful that your feet aren't sticking out. Wiser not to risk another shout.' This point shows that he is thinking clearly and with cunning: he realises that if the seekers are quite close they will be able to locate him from the direction of his voice. While he waits, the child tries to calm himself down, as he speaks to himself and tries to work out the state of the game. 'They'll probably be searching the bushes near the swing.'

The child's state is now marked by anxiety, as he realises that even the slightest movement might reveal his whereabouts: 'And here they are, whispering at the door; you've never heard them sound so hushed before. Don't breathe. Don't move. Stay dumb. Hide in your blindness.' The staccato commands, as if made by an inner voice, emphasise the drama of this crucial moment of potential discovery: his heart beats fast and powerfully, like the pounding rhythm of the monosyllables.

Once the child has evaded discovery for a while, Vernon Scannell gives the reader the strong impression that the child becomes very proud of his achievement in avoiding being found: 'They must be thinking you're very clever, getting more puzzled as they search all over.' The voice tempts him to feel self-satisfied, as he imagines the admiration of the rest of the group.

However, this confident pride cannot last, and as time passes new emotions start to affect the child. Although he thinks the others must be puzzled, it is his turn to start to wonder what is happening. The length of the wait now affects him, to the point where he now feels lonely: he has hidden for a very long time, and the mental uncertainty is creeping over him, together with the physical sensations which arise from his lengthy stay in one place: 'It seems a long time since they went away. Your legs are stiff, the cold bites through your coat; the dark damp smell of sand moves in your throat.'

Once the child makes the decision to emerge from his hiding-place, and announce to the rest of them that he is the victor, the initial mood of excitement returns, as he anticipates their recognition of his triumph: 'It's time to let them know that you're the winner.' Having been confined to a virtual prison, he now feels a wave of relief at being able to break free. Now, the inner voice, instead of bidding him stay in a frozen state, urges him to action. All the physical aching and mental uncertainties are banished: 'Push off the sacks. Uncurl and stretch. That's better.' Not only is the tension released, but his whole body springs back to life. He is triumphant, and his words, the first in direct speech since the opening line, convey the sense of victory: 'I've won! Here I am! Come and own up I've caught you!'. Instead of being 'caught', he sees himself as the captor.

His subsequent emotional state has to be imagined. Scannell does not need to spell out the bitter sense of anti-climax, disappointment and betrayal which now come over him. The sense that he is a victim of a grand conspiracy is underlined by the actions of nature: not only the other children are silent: even inanimate objects 'hold their breath'. The effect of the final, taunting question is overwhelming. The lack of losers not only makes the victory hollow, but creates a sense that the universe is unfair: what can he rely on if the rules of this ancient game are broken? The poem ends with an ironic twist: he, for whom they have been seeking, now has nothing left but to try to find the seekers.

Example 3: Leaving School (Williams)

- **How do the child's feelings about school change over time?**

Note the key words in the question: **feelings**, **school**, **change**.
   - Make sure you show how the child feels about the events he experiences;
   - Deal with the changes over the time he is at the school;
   - Look at the poet's **choice of words**.

Model Answer

The start of the poem announces a bold beginning to a big adventure. At the tender age of eight, the boy leaves home to explore 'the world', clad, like an adult, in a 'grey flannel suit'. His feelings about this adventure are clear: there is none of the apprehensiveness which might be expected at such a moment: 'I thought it was going to be fun'. However, the words 'I thought' perhaps present the first hint that everything is not going to turn out as well as he hoped.

The next scene shows the boy at the school, when the first sets of instructions are being given out to the new pupils. We learn that he did not take in the instructions because he 'wasn't listening'. But we do not know why: perhaps he was so excited about the new environment that he simply could not concentrate; or possibly he was so confident that he did not feel that he even needed to listen, since he knew it all. He quickly learnt that things were not necessarily going to be so straightforward, by the fact that he 'didn't have any sheets' for his bed. It is not difficult to imagine that this would have marked him out as different right from the start: we know how cruel young boys can be to the odd one out.

His failure to adjust to school routine was shown also by his getting lost. The headmaster's wife's attempts to turn the experience into an exciting game was doubtless well-intentioned, but may not have been entirely successful, since the boy remained out of his depth and confused, one of the battleships which was sunk, perhaps. This confusion was shown by the fact that he could not even get the uniform right: 'wearing the wrong shoes'.

In the second stanza, the boy elaborates on the increasing sense of disorientation and inability to cope with boarding school life which he experienced. The only thing he enjoyed, it appears, was the waiting. This may have been because at least while waiting for things to happen he was not being faced with his inadequacies, as he clearly was in his lessons. Reading classes exposed his weaknesses particularly sharply, since he had thought himself a confident reader, but now realised that this was only because he confined himself to what was already familiar to him. His inability to make progress with the 'Beacon Series', a reading course which the class was clearly expected to speed through, resulted in a sense of ignorance: 'I don't know'. Ignorance led to a further withdrawal: he became silent in all his classes. The sense of not coping with routine activities evidently increased, as was shown by his constant failure to 'hang something up'. In this stanza, by focusing on small instances in simple language, the poet has managed to create a real feeling of helplessness: the boy's intellectual failings were made worse by an inability to do things properly. The impression is that, in a school so well-organised and disciplined, such failures were particularly significant.

He became, in the final stanza, aware just how remote the school environment was from his home: he felt 'so far away from home', both physically and in his feelings. The forgetfulness became still worse, and led to failures to do even the simplest things which, before he went away to school, would have presented him with no difficulty. The breakdown is presented again in simple language, perhaps with a touch of humour, self-mocking: 'I forgot how to get undressed'. The next event, when the headmaster's wife came to inspect the class, takes things one step further, with a surprising line: 'I was fully dressed again, ready for bed'. This suggests something more than a failure to take his clothes off in the right order, and the reader wonders why he is fully dressed, and whether the headmaster's wife realised, since she was concentrating on a minor offence of not having cleaned his teeth. The last line picks up the start of the poem, and shows him now undertaking a journey in the opposite direction, leaving the school, again with his suitcase. But the ending lacks a full explanation. Did he slip out of the school at night? Did he really leave, or was he 'miles away' only in his mind, wishing himself somewhere else? Whichever it is, the sadness and despair of the situation are all too clear, despite the lack of strong vocabulary to describe his feelings. The poem has captured, with its short sentences, simple language and sharp images, a real sense of what a frightening, bewildering experience it can be to go away to boarding school.

Glossary of poetic terms

The following list gives a definition and example of each of the most common terms you will meet when reading or writing about poetry:

Alliteration – The repetition of consonants, especially at the start of successive words: *summer gloves and satin sandals* (Joseph: 'Warning')

Assonance – The repetition of the same vowel sound (a,e,i,o,u) in close succession: *gold-rolled cigarette* (Soyinka: 'Telephone Conversation')

Dramatic Monologue – The poet writes in the voice of a particular character (adopts the 'persona' of someone else): the three sections of 'Not My Best Side' (Fanthorpe)

Enjambement – The meaning of the poem runs straight on to the next line. This can help a sense of continuity in the writing. Sometimes, just one or two words are held over, which may then receive greater emphasis: frequent occurrences, well worth studying, in 'You Will Be Hearing From Us Shortly' (Fanthorpe)

Hyperbole – An exaggeration for dramatic effect: *national disaster* (Fanthorpe: 'Dear Mr Lee')

Imagery – The general term for pictures made with words, such as comparisons made with similes and metaphors.

Metaphor – The poet compares one object with another directly, without using *like* or *as*: *I am only a cloud* (Fanthorpe: 'Old Man, Old Man')

Metre – The pattern of stressed and unstressed syllables in a line of poetry.

Onomatopoeia – The actual sound made by someone or something is recreated in the sound of the word: *clockface…. click… clockless… tickless* (Fanthorpe: 'Half-past Two')

Personification – An object or a quality is described as if it were a person or possessing human qualities: *The bushes hold their breath* (Scannell: 'Hide and Seek')

Rhythm – The movement of the metre through the pattern of stressed and unstressed syllables.

Simile – A comparison introduced with words such as like or as: *The sacks… smell like the seaside* (Scannell: 'Hide and Seek')

Sonnet – A poem of fourteen lines.

Stanza – A verse of poetry.

Theme – A subject which is important within a poem. There may be one main theme or several, some more important than others: old age, school, confusion…

Tone – The way in which a writer or speaker conveys feelings, attitudes or intentions.

non-fiction

Introduction: at the crossroads

What happens when we arrive at a crossroads?

We have to make a decision – to decide which way to go. Crossroads can be puzzling places. They need us to choose between different possibilities – sometimes several of them. We may feel very uncertain, because we are not sure what will lie at the end of each road.

Even if there are signposts, these will tell us only a name, and not what it is like when we arrive there. This is as true of the journey of life as it is when we are walking or driving somewhere. Much of the time we may travel on, not worrying too much about the direction we are going in, or which way to go next. But sometimes we are faced with a real moment of decision about the course of our life. The selection in *Tracks 2* has been made in such a way as to look closely at such times, which may include:

○ birth and death;

○ marriage or divorce;

○ starting school or leaving school;

○ an important meeting.

The idea is to look at how the writers explore the significance of events like these. As the American poet Robert Frost put it:

Two roads diverged in a wood, and I –
I took the one less travelled by,
And that has made all the difference.

In studying these texts, which deal with different writers' experiences of reaching 'the crossroads', think about:

○ how, in writing about these experiences, they have tried to make sense of what was happening to them;

○ how they reached important decisions and what they decided to do;

○ how you have reacted, or would react, if faced with similar circumstances.

Big School, Big Trauma and Starting School

The start of the school year

These two articles were written in the same newspaper, *The Independent*, on the same day, as part of that paper's coverage of the start of the new school year, looking particularly at those starting secondary school. In the first, the journalist, Celia Dodd, looks at the fact that this can be a difficult time for children and considers what can be done about it. In the second, a boy aged 11, James Bateson, describes his own thoughts and feelings.

The title of the first article, 'Big School, Big Trauma', suggests strongly that it can be a very disturbing and unsettling time and experience. The word 'trauma' is the Greek word for a 'wound' or injury', and its use suggests something that can affect people, even hurt them, deeply. Nowadays, to be 'traumatised' is to experience a strong psychological shock. Not everyone reacts identically to such events, however. For some, transferring to a new school is just a magical experience, exciting and eagerly looked forward to.

Changing School

Why is it that moving from primary to secondary school is such a big step? The table below suggests a few of the differences between many primary and secondary schools.

Primary school	Secondary School
Mostly one class teacher	Many different teachers
One building and small grounds	Several buildings, with large playing-fields
Most lessons in one place	Much moving between lessons
Close to home	Further away
Friends you've known a long time	Many new people to get to know
You receive much help and guidance	You have to take more responsibility

You may be able to add to this list, or some of these may not be true for you. For each item on your revised list, think about how you feel about the differences. You could mark a tick for those you liked and a cross for any that you disliked or which worried you. If others in the class are also doing this, you may wish to compare their lists and answers with yours, to see how differently or similarly different members of the class reacted. Are there any patterns which emerge particularly strongly?

Comparing the two articles

The most obvious difference is that one article is written by a journalist, the other by a child. But it is possible to compare the articles in other ways, too. The following are some of the ways in which you may wish to make comparisons:

- The writer's viewpoint on the subject
- The way the subject is handled
- The argument which is offered
- The use of language
- The attitude towards the reader
- The understanding of young people's feeling
- The tone of the writing

Using such headings, and any others of your own choosing, analyse closely the way in which you respond to the two articles.

- Which do you find more interesting and convincing?

Easing the transition

Every year, many thousands of young people move from junior to senior school, usually at the age of 11. The articles which you have studied suggest a number of ways in which this can be a difficult experience.

- Imagine that you have been asked to put to the head teacher of a secondary school a number of suggestions for improving the arrangements and making life easier and more comfortable for the pupils. Produce a brief summary of up to FIVE things which you feel could be done to make pupils' life easier and better at this stage. One suggestion is offered to start your thinking:
- ○ Each Year 6 pupil should be visited by a Year 7 pupil from the chosen secondary school, who would be able to answer any questions about the new school.

Black Boy

'Black Boy' deals with the themes of **violence** and **bullying**.

Although the boy is seen to be a black boy, it is not stated in this extract that he is beaten up because he is black. However, from the title it seems likely that the gang was a gang of white youths, and therefore it is quite possible that the reason for his being beaten up is connected with the colour of his skin. Certainly, much street violence both in America and in Britain is racially motivated. The newspapers in England in 2001 had many references to the fighting on the streets of Oldham, Lancashire, between groups of white youths and those of Asian background.

All that we know from the text is that the boy lives with his mother and brother, since his father has left home, for reasons which are not stated. In the absence of his father, the boy has to take on more of the responsibility for the family, including help with the shopping.

Analysing the language

To begin to analyse the extract, it may be helpful to divide it into a number of stages. These may be summarised in the following way:

- Setting the scene – background information
- The first encounter with the gang of boys
- His mother's reaction – sends him out again
- His fear of going out – his mother's insistence
- The second encounter
- His mother's reaction – gives him a stick and sends him out again
- His attempt to avoid going out
- Her continued insistence, accompanied by threats
- His choice (the 'crossroads') – he decides to go
- The victory over his enemies
- His realisation that he has won.

To continue the analysis, consider the language which is used to build up the effect. One way of doing this is to look at the different kinds of word ('parts of speech') used to build up the description. In particular, there is the writer's use of **verbs**, **nouns**, **adjectives** and **adverbs**.

In the first stage, for example, some of the key words are:

- **Setting the scene – background information**

Verbs	Nouns	Adjectives	Adverbs
left	despair	alone	solemnly
cry	dread	tired	
		dispirited	
		frightened	

From these words, it is easy to see how the writer creates a rather unhappy, anxious atmosphere and shows that the life of the family is not an easy one. The words are even more striking in the last-but-one stage, after he decided to go out and face the gang once more.

○ **The victory over his enemies**

Verbs		Nouns	Adjectives	Adverbs
walked	lamming	fear	blind	slowly
breathe	fought	fear	cold	tightly
surrounded	lay low	stick	clenched	scarcely
grab	knock	skull	stark	again
kill	kill	skull		again
threatened	strike back	tears		
closed in	flayed	teeth		
let fly	throw	fear		
crack	hit	strength		
swung	scattered	blow		
yelling	tore	frenzy		
nursing	screaming	disbelief		

This summary underlines how much dramatic action and strong emotion there is in this final confrontation: note especially the large number of violent 'action' verbs close to each other.

The characters

Apart from the unnamed gang of boys, the only two characters who feature strongly in the extract are the boy's mother and the boy himself. Think about how each is portrayed and your reactions to these two characters.

Think about

The decisions which were made by the boy and by the mother:

○ Was there a particular 'crossroads' moment for the boy?

○ If you had been the mother, how would you have handled the situation?

○ If you had been the boy, would you have acted as he did?

The issues the writer is inviting us to explore:

○ Violence on the streets.

○ The behaviour of gangs of youths.

○ What it is like to be the victim.

○ How parents can help children who are on the receiving end of violence or bullying.

○ How children can learn even from the unpleasant things that happen to them.

○ Growing up as a black person in a society such as this.

Find opportunities to discuss with your friends

○ Have any of you had to cope with bullying?

○ If so, did you manage to find a way of doing so successfully, so that the bullying stopped, and were you helped by any other people (friends, parents, teachers, other grown-ups, other children)?

○ What should you do if you come across incidents of violent bullying or name-calling at school? Is it right to tell an adult such as a teacher, or would that be telling tales? If we don't tell an adult, how are we going to stop it?

Fenland Chronicle

This extract is one of a number of 'first person' memories about life in the early part of the twentieth century. The scene is set in the county of Norfolk. The part of England known as 'Fenland' or 'The Fens' covers much of East Anglia. It is generally very flat, low-lying countryside.

The story was narrated by a woman looking back over her life to when she and her friends were young. She did not write it down herself; it was an oral account in which she told her story out loud, with a recorder switched on so that it could be written down later by someone else. The writer tried to be true to the way that the woman spoke by writing in her regional (Norfolk) dialect.

In some ways, the events described seem a very long time ago. It feels like a different country in terms of the way in which children were treated, the living and working conditions and the general attitudes. Yet there are still people alive today who remember such things.

Contrasts between then and now

This extract is placed after a number of passages which deal with children growing up today, looking at significant events in their lives, whether connected with school or home life and the streets. The 'crossroad' moment for these young girls was being sent away, just as it was for the boy in 'Leaving School'. The girls were older than he was when they had to leave home, but what they faced was a particularly hard life, lacking even the comforts of a boarding school. The extract gives a strong picture of the conditions they had to face, and the narrator makes it very clear that this was not a life which was easy to endure. She makes a number of points about the girls' **age, conditions, pay, social and family life.**
The following are some of the main points:

- Girls were often sent into service as young as eleven.
- They had to leave their family completely.
- They often had to live many miles away from their family.
- They were often treated worse than a dog.
- The farmers had no idea how to look after the girls.
- They took advantage of people's poverty to take their children from them.
- They regarded them as slaves.
- The girls hardly received any wages.
- The working hours were extremely long.
- The conditions in which they worked could be terrible.

Think about

- The differences between being sent away to school and being sent away into service.
- The feelings of the parents who sent their girls away into service.
- The worst features of being in service (were there any consolations?)
- How being sent to 'good service' in a grand house would have differed from the experience of the girls from the Fens.
- What has changed in our society and legal system to help protect young people from being treated as 'slaves'.

○ The fact that there are still parts of the world where the young are not treated any better than the Fenland girls. (Why is this? What will need to happen to change the lives of those young people?)

Shady's Life

Using the evidence from this extract, try to construct a timetable for a day in Shady's life. Very few times of day are stated, so you will have to make some guesses. The list could start:

> 6.00 am   *Wake up (earlier on churning days).*

Read through the answer to the question about Shady which is given on page 52. Can you think of other points you would have wished to make in answering this question?

'First person' accounts

Personal recollections are obviously an important kind of historical source, which you may well be studying as part of a history course. In addition, they can also be powerful to read because they tell personal stories, convey strong emotions, or explore ideas and attitudes. Think about:

○ What it is that the narrator of this account feels strongly about, and why.
○ How her way of telling the story helps you to understand the events.
○ The importance of the details which she recalls in conveying the conditions of the girls' lives.
○ What else you would need to know in order to have a full picture of these events (for example, the thoughts of those employing the girls).
○ How the use of dialect affects your response to the narrative (find examples).
○ The narrator's distinction between 'good' and 'bad' service.
○ How easy (or hard) it is to tell the facts apart from the narrator's own opinions. (Is there bias in favour of the girls and against their employers?)
○ What is your own response to the lives of the girls? Why do you react in this way?

A farmer's view

'I perform a valuable service in this community by giving young girls experience of employment for a couple of years. If they do well with me, they can better themselves, perhaps by working in the fine household of a local landowner. And if I did not offer them work, their poor parents and they might end up starving, because there is nothing else for them to do. Yes, I work them hard, but that is how they will learn to be good workers afterwards. You may not think five pounds for a year's work is very much, but I keep them fed and clothed. Apart from anything else, they'd be no use to me if they were sick and hungry, so I make sure they come to no harm. They learn many valuable crafts with me, and they leave me ready to take their chances in the world.'

How convincing a case does this (imaginary) farmer make here?

Notes from a Small Island

Why does the book have this title?

Usually, the first thing we find out about a book is its title. Titles are often very carefully chosen in order to tempt the reader and also to convey some impression. You may be able to think of some book titles which you found memorable.

The first word is '**Notes**'. When we write notes, they are often written in a kind of 'shorthand', not necessarily even in full sentences. You may well have written revision notes, for example. Other notes are to remind you of something you might forget. Or they are to help you put your thoughts in order, in preparation for writing them up more fully at a later stage. 'Notes' therefore suggests some 'jottings' which are rather slight, possibly unfinished: imagine the difference if he had used, for example, '**Essay**', '**Reflections**' or '**Memoirs**'.

The other key words are '**Small Island**'. We wonder about this, too. Why not '**The British Isles**', or '**England**', or '**Great Britain**'? Why emphasise that this is a *small* country, why that it is an *island*? Is the author suggesting that this place is rather insignificant, and that it is rather 'insular' (isolated, or cut off)?

At least the title starts us thinking. So does the idea of beginning with a 'prologue', rather than straight in with Chapter One. Prologues usually belong in plays – Shakespeare used them, for example. Their purpose in plays is also to start people thinking. They set the scene, establish the mood, and may introduce the main characters and themes. So it is reasonable to expect that this prologue will help to get the reader into the swing of things, and give us something of a feel for the kind of story we are in for.

What is the book about?

We do in fact learn various things from the prologue. It tells us:

○ That the book will be written in first person narrative – it is, in fact, autobiographical.

○ It is about a traveller from France who arrives in England. It seems to be the story of the narrator's journeys, therefore – it is reasonable to assume that it is a travel book of some kind.

○ The narrator seems rather accident-prone – things do not always work out for him.

○ He is an acute observer – of both people and landscapes.

○ He writes with wit and humour, and can tell a funny story, with a clever turn of phrase.

○ He seems to some extent to make fun of the English (and the French).

Of course, these clues might be deceptive (although those who have read the whole book will know that they are not). At any rate, the prologue does fulfil some of the purposes suggested above.

What is Bill Bryson's writing like?

Bill Bryson's writing has been widely admired, and this book remains an extremely popular one, having been high in the 'best-sellers' charts for several years. In order to try to understand what it is that makes his writing work so well, it may be helpful to analyse closely two parts of the extract.

'Only the previous day, I had handed over an exceptionally plump wad of colourful francs to a beady-eyed Picardy hotelier in payment for one night in a lumpy bed and a plate of mysterious chasseur containing the bones of assorted small animals, much of which had to be secreted away in a large napkin in order not to appear impolite, and had determined thenceforth to be more cautious with expenditures.'

'The world was bathed in that milky pre-dawn light that seems to come from nowhere. Gulls wheeled and cried over the water. Beyond them, past the stone breakwater, a ferry, vast and well lit, slid regally out to sea.'

WANTED
BILL BRYSON
A reward will be offered for information leading to the discovery of this man

In the first (on page 46) he is recalling an event before he left France for England, so on this occasion his humour is not connected with the English but with the French. This can be contrasted with the very different effects achieved in the description opposite.

The second passage, like the first one, is marked by the use of telling detail. However, here Bryson is not seeking to make fun – of the English, the French, or anyone. The effect of the description is to enable the reader to picture the scene, almost as though it were a painting or, say, a black and white photograph. Yet it is not only a picture: it is one presented with a sense of affection or appreciation for the scene. It is as if Bryson feels that, having shown that he can write with a good sense of humour, he needs to demonstrate that he can also write in a more serious style. And also it seems to suggest that he has not come to England only to have some fun at the expense of the English, but with a mind open to enjoy and respond to the place he is visiting. If English readers so far have felt that this American visitor is only out for a joke, this passage alerts us to the fact that there is warmth in his feelings about the country. This becomes very clear later in the book, in fact. Bill Bryson liked England so much that he stayed for nearly twenty years.

What is Bill Bryson himself really like?
The prologue offers a number of clues about Bill Bryson, but without very much detail.
- Suppose that you had only this prologue to go on, think about the statement you would be able to compile in response to the above advertisement.
- Check all the evidence carefully.
- Try to give as much information as you can about him, especially his character.

Think about
- The writer's use of vocabulary and skill at choosing words. (Pick out some examples which seem to you particularly effective.)
- The writer's ability to describe a scene or event.
- The effect of the occasional use of dialogue.
- The writer's ability to laugh at himself.
- The kinds of thing and people that he finds amusing.

Discuss
- Would you want to read the rest of the book?
- (If you have, tell others what you thought of it.)
- Is the sense of humour cruel or well-meaning?
- Does the writer have any serious points to make?
- Does his description of Dover seem to you to be a good one?
- Is it, for example, accurate, objective, exaggerated, well-observed, biased?
- What kind of book is most useful for helping you understand what a country is really like?

Seize the Moment

Looking Down

The picture on the left is a view of the earth from space. It is, quite literally, out of this world. Astronauts are the only people who can have this view, although we can share it to some extent through television and photography. They become able to look down on the earth and everyone on it. Those of us unable to go into space still often seek vantage-points from which to look down on the earth. Some such viewpoints are:

flight by aeroplane   top of a mountain   the 'London Eye'
the Empire State Building   hot-air balloons   stands in a sports stadium.

Think about why people want to be able to look down on things. Some possibilities are:

- It gives the best **overview** – a panorama.
- You can feel as though you are **set apart** from everything and everyone.
- There is a different **perspective** on everything.
- Being higher up can give one a sense of **superiority**.

Something of these feelings certainly comes through from what Helen Sharman writes (below the photograph).

'I could see the curvature of the Earth! Speckly white clouds! A Brilliant azure sea… Dreams sometimes do come true and I felt so alive!'

and a little later:

'Just eight minutes ago I had been bound to the Earth's surface, now I was in space. Eight minutes ago my family had been less than a mile away from me; now we were not even on the same planet.'

Counting down

But before reaching such a view, there is the take-off, and particularly the waiting for take-off. Even though we have not experienced the countdown to a space flight, we have probably all counted down the minutes and seconds to some important event, such as:

- the start of a race;
- the take-off of an aeroplane;
- the beginning or end of an examination.

Countdowns can be very tense events. You can perhaps recall your feelings about one. These may have included some or all of the following:

suspense   anticipation   fear   excitement   nerves   anxiety

For Helen Sharman, too, the countdown was clearly an important 'crossroads' moment. She tells us very little directly about what she felt before take-off, but she recalled every detail of the moments before it happened, including every little **movement**, **sight** or **sound**. Every second was counted, and there was not just the initial take-off to undergo: there were countdowns to the separation of the escape rocket and the booster rockets, and the ditching of the second and third stage. Each second was, clearly, vital. The title 'Seize the Moment' is itself significant. It emphasises

- what an amazing opportunity Helen Sharman felt she had, which had to be grasped eagerly;
- the importance of each individual moment when you are journeying into space;
- that some moments were so precious that she wanted to try to capture them and keep them for ever; however, the essence of a moment is that it cannot be caught and kept. It is gone before you can begin to seize it, and the next moment has arrived.

Breaking down

A successful space launch depends on the rocket scientists' solving large numbers of detailed, technical problems. To do this successfully means **breaking down** (analysing) the problem into its different parts. The spacecraft also had to be 'broken down' into its parts. From all the huge rocket that left the launching-pad, only one comparatively small section was left by the end of the extract. The separation of the stages really marked the stages of the journey into weightlessness, and it is possible to examine the astronaut's feelings and actions at each stage in the journey. Then, at the experience of weightlessness, all the normal rules seemed to break down, and the laws of gravity were defied:

'*The talisman was no longer tense against its string. It hovered by the hatch, the string snaking loosely towards it. It had suddenly become, as we had suddenly become, weightless.*'

Science and magic, fantasy and reality

This extract contains a number of contrasts which can be explored through the writer's **language** and **ideas**.

The passage deals with **science** and **magic**, which are often seen as the opposite of each other, but not necessarily. Helen Sharman makes it clear that a successful space voyage is the product of the precise application of **mathematics, science and technology**. Absolute accuracy is essential: there is no place for guesswork or emotion when launching a spaceship. Her descriptions bring home, with their **technical language** (*g-forces, protective fairing, acceleration*), that this is a scientific account. But magic and fantasy are also present, with language that is almost **poetic** in its power, while still based entirely on the writer's actual observations and sensations:

Sunlight streamed in; diamond-studded clouds; the string snaking loosely.
The contrast is shown above all in the repeated reference to the ***talisman***. This is perhaps the most surprising and unexpected thing to find, but it is mentioned not once but four times.

- What is your reaction to learning that the scientists aboard the spaceship had a lucky charm?
- Why do you think Helen Sharman refers to it so often?
- What is its importance in the passage?

Men and women

Most astronauts have been men. Helen Sharman is the only British woman to have been into space.

- Do you think men and women have different reactions to such events?
- Would you have been at all surprised to find that the writer was a man?
- How effective do you find the mixture of technical and poetic language, science and magic, in bringing to life the experience of an astronaut making her first journey into space?
- What do you think you would feel about making such a journey? (Discuss your reactions with your friends, noting any similarities and differences.)

Dictionary definition

talisman an object supposed to be endowed with magic powers, especially of averting evil from or bringing good luck to its holder.

Inform, explain, describe: pointers for Question 3

The GCSE Syllabus sets out a number of ways of writing, which are assessed in different parts of the syllabus and examination.

○ Question 3 on Papers 2F and 4H is designed to test candidates' ability to write according to the **range of writing:** inform, explain, describe.

○ The topics set for this question ask writers to **use and adapt for specific purpose**.

The stimulus material from *Tracks 2* provides non-fiction content on which candidates may draw in their writing.

○ Make sure that your writing covers properly what is required.

○ You will find it helpful to think about the three words in turn, and look at the differences between them.

Inform

To **inform** means to tell someone something, to pass on **information**. Think about the qualities of a good informant who must be able to:

○ present the information clearly;

○ communicate facts accurately;

○ help a reader to appreciate exactly what has happened.

Setting out your information well, whether in speaking or in writing, is one of the secrets of effective communication. It needs:

○ a clear head;

○ a logical mind;

○ good organisation;

○ effective use of language;

○ a good grasp of facts – and figures, where appropriate.

Explain

To **explain** is to go a step further than simply informing. A good **explanation** is one which enables a listener or reader to understand, so when explaining it is necessary to:

○ understand the topic fully – what the problem is, how something works, why something has happened;

○ find ways of putting over the points so that any difficulties are sorted out, and any confusion cleared up;

○ use a variety of means to deal with the need for technical explanations or clarifications. A good explanation leaves the reader or listener clear, satisfied and free from doubt.

Describe

To **describe** is a kind of drawing in words. You may be asked to describe an object, a person, a scene or a series of events. A good **description** has the qualities of a good photograph or portrait. You can imagine that, if you have seen a crime being committed, the police will be very grateful for any **information**, and for an **explanation** of what has taken place. But a **description** of a place, an action or – especially – a person will be the most effective way of leading to an arrest. When describing, it is necessary to:

○ use vivid, graphic words which will help someone to picture something or someone clearly;

○ give as much relevant information as possible, as well as a general, overall description;

○ be prepared to use images, including metaphors and similes;

○ make sure that your reader or listener can follow clearly what you are saying;

○ check that you have conveyed the fullest possible account.

Non-fiction specimen questions: Questions 2 and 3 (2F/4H)

Question 2

Big School, Big Trauma and Starting School

- Both of these articles suggest that the change from primary to secondary school can cause children to be very anxious or insecure. Use the ideas and information from these two articles to show the main reasons why children may have such fears.
- What do these articles suggest that schools should do to make new pupils feel welcome?

Black Boy

- Explain how the writer's mother reacted to the boy's experience of bullying and show what the effect of her advice was on him.
- How does the writer's language emphasise the violence of the incidents described?

Fenland Chronicle

- What does the extract show about the advantages and disadvantages of sending young girls away 'to service'?
- What do we learn about the conditions and experiences of 'Shady' while she was working in service?

Notes from a Small Island

- What aspects of England struck Bill Bryson most strongly when he first arrived, and why?
- In what ways does Bill Bryson add humour to his description of events?

Seize the Moment

- How much do we learn from this extract about Helen Sharman's feelings on her first space expedition?
- Show how Helen Sharman's language enables us to sense her physical feelings at the different stages described in the passage.

Question 3

In this question, you may be able to make reference to some of the ideas from 'At the crossroads', but you may also draw on information and ideas from other sources and from your own experience.

- 'Childhood: the happiest days of your life'. Write a magazine article in which you explain why you think this was true or untrue of your life up to the age of 11.
- Imagine that you have run away from home or school. Write a letter to a friend or member of your family explaining why you took this decision and what your life has been like.
- Place yourself in the position of someone being interviewed EITHER for a place in a sixth form or further education college OR for a first job. Write a diary account in which you record your thoughts and feelings before, during and after the interview.
- Write a letter to an elderly person (such as a grandparent) in which you set out your hopes and fears for the future.
- Write a letter to the local newspaper explaining what you think should be done to prevent EITHER prejudice to different groups of people OR violence and disorderly behaviour on the streets.

Model answers: Question 2

- **What do we learn about the conditions and experiences of 'Shady' while she was working in service?**

It is difficult for us today to imagine the kind of life 'Shady' lived, as a girl sent away at the age of thirteen, but Sybil Marshall's account in 'Fenland Chronicle' recaptures these events with detailed clarity. She begins by painting a scene of isolation: the big, solitary house was almost like a prison, from which 'there was no escape'.

The routine which Shady experienced must, however, often have made her desperately keen to escape. The work was endless, with a wide range of tasks, the hours were extremely long and the conditions most unpleasant. There were very few compensations. Any slip could clearly lead to dismissal, since we are told that 'if she behaved herself and stuck it out a whole year' she would earn a year's wages of five pounds.

The length of Shady's working day is emphasised from the start of the description of her duties: 'She were woke up at 6 a.m.... she had to get up straight away.' Later, the author mentions that on some days, 'churning days', the start was even earlier. Although the account does not state exactly how long the working day was, it is stressed that 'she had no time off at all during the day' and there is a list of the duties she had to perform after supper. Evidently she might sometimes have a little time before going to bed, but very little.

The hard, unpleasant nature of the work is also made very clear from the account. The huge, old-fashioned kitchen range was obviously both difficult to light and extremely hard work to keep clean. Without modern equipment, cleaning was always an arduous task, especially the scrubbing of the tiles on the kitchen floor, described as 'a terrible job' because of its size and the lack of hot water. For Shady, when she at last finished this job there was no relief, since the cleaning of the dairy was just as forbidding a task. As the account continues, it is easy to see just what was expected of Shady: making tea and breakfast, washing up, housework — the daily round was relentless.

To keep her going through all this, you would have thought that Shady would need a nourishing diet, rich in protein and vitamins. Yet the only food which is mentioned for her was 'bread and butter'. The physical conditions in which she worked made matters still worse: the lack of light and the coldness of the house are underlined, with the graphic reference to the water freezing on the kitchen floor before it could be mopped up. A final indignity was to have to put up with being in close proximity to the 'old shepherd', with whom 'no decent girl were safe'. This hints at the strong possibility of sexual abuse to which such young girls were subjected. The only reference to Shady's own feelings is her dread of having to sit with him.

Generally, Sybil Marshall recounts Shady's life in a matter-of-fact, vivid style, with only occasional suggestions about how difficult it was. The writer is keen to stress that there was a big difference between being sent to what she calls 'good service', which she regards as a perfectly reasonable fate for a young girl, and the kind of experience which Shady and others like her had to undergo. Shady, like Eva, who is mentioned earlier in the passage, was exploited in a cruel manner, evidently treated no better than the animals with which she was obliged to spend much of her time.

● **In what ways does Bill Bryson add humour to his description of events?**

Bill Bryson spends much of the time laughing at himself for the mistakes and misunderstanding of situations which he makes. However, he also pokes gentle fun at the English and French, and sometimes creates humour simply by the detailed description of the absurd things which happen to him.

The prologue starts with a straightforward description of the sight which greeted him on arrival in England. The 'fog', which no doubt many foreigners associate with England, is mentioned, but there is nothing immediately to suggest a humorous account. The first hint of humour comes from his imagined words to a guesthouse owner, which contains some more stereotypical snippets of Englishness: the roast beef, pickle and beer. It is also amusing that he imagines himself saying that he will not have anything to eat and then accepting a lavish snack. All this builds up a picture of arriving safely at a warm and welcoming establishment. What happened next shattered that dream in a number of ways: first, his foreignness is stressed by his falling over the doorstep and crashing into milk bottles (a strange discovery in itself to American eyes). Secondly, the tone of the person to whom he spoke was hardly one of welcome. And thirdly, he became rapidly aware that English English and American English are not identical, with his misunderstanding of the phrase 'on the front'. A similar confusion occurs later on when the words 'transport caff' are taken by him to be a 'transport calf'.

By this time, we realise that the author's arrival is not going to go smoothly, and are prepared from more comical escapades. The account of the French meal, consisting of assorted rodents, which he had to hide in a napkin, is told partly to emphasise that he has very little money, and hence cannot afford to stay in a decent hotel. The tale of his night attempting to sleep inside a seaside shelter is a mixture of sad and humorous elements. We sympathise with Bill Bryson for the uncomfortable conditions, the cold and the noises which keep him awake. But this sad tale is told with a definite sense of humour, as the narrative of his dreams is full of weird things, as the French cook takes revenge on him for despising his food. Also, he paints an amusing picture of his appearance as he struggles to keep warm, with the boxer shorts acting as a 'desperate headwarmer'.

Bryson's skilful use of language enables us to picture events in a memorable way, such as the description of the woman at the guesthouse as a 'silhouette with hair curlers', the reference to the dog which 'wasn't so much walking as being dragged along on three legs', and saying that the sky 'looked like a pile of wet towels'. The conversation with the man walking the dog has its amusing moments, too. The man's sense of optimism about the weather forecast enables the author to make more fun of the English weather, and the English obsession with it. Up to this point, we have probably not been aware that he has forgotten to take the underpants off his head, but the man's polite pointing out of this fact and his embarrassed reaction show strongly that he can laugh at himself. We also note with amusement his attempts to ensure that the dog does not succeed as it strains 'desperately to moisten' his leg. The passage ends with a development of the joke about the English weather, as the man's statement that it is 'definitely brightening up' is undermined immediately by the first spots of rain.

From this opening, we have already obtained a clear impression of the kind of narrative with which the writer is going to present us. It will have, no doubt, scenes of genuine appreciation, such as the fine description of the coast before dawn broke. It will be a series of adventures in which some of his stereotypes of English life may be confirmed but others will be contradicted. Also, he will appear as a friendly but impoverished American, stumbling around this new country in a state of confusion. The prologue is thus most effective in setting the scene and in inviting the reader to share in the writer's travels.

Model answers: Question 3

- **Write a letter to an elderly person (such as a grandparent) in which you set out your hopes and fears for the future.**

Dear Grandma,

Today is your eightieth birthday, and I want to wish you a very happy day. I thought that this would be a good time to share my thoughts about the future, since I hope to be able to look forward to a long and varied life, as you have been able to do.

At the start of the twenty-first century, many things must seem so different from when you were a girl. Things are changing so fast, and in many ways it is impossible for me to imagine what life will be like in sixty-five years' time. One thing is for sure. Many more people will be able to live long, healthy lives. Who knows? We may live to be well over a hundred! Not that I am sure I would wish for that. I feel that there is a danger that medical science will interfere too much with nature, and I am really worried about what may happen with genetic engineering and other technological advances.

These technological changes have the capacity to enrich our lives greatly. But I feel it is just as important, if not more so, to hold on to the lessons which we have learnt from your generation about what really matters: love, friendship, health, music, books and a good home, for example. As to the last of these, I remember you telling me what it was like when you grew up without central heating, regular hot water, washing machines or televisions. It is difficult for us to imagine such a life now, but there are still people in other parts of the world who live like this. My hope is that in the future all countries will have a decent standard of living and that world poverty will be a thing of the past.

Not only work in the home, but the whole pattern of employment is changing. We have been told by our careers advisers that few of us will have a single 'job for life'. I know that I must be versatile and adaptable, and need to develop useful skills. I look forward to a long working life. Who knows? Perhaps we shall be able to work for three or four days each week, continuing well into our seventies. If so, then we shall certainly have time to take advantage of increasing opportunities to travel, both on this planet and perhaps further afield.

You and grandad have been married for nearly sixty years. You have told me that your marriage vows were promises made for life. The divorce statistics horrify you, I know. Many changes to family life are emerging in our society, but I can see that the stability and care which you gave to my mother and her brothers have stood them in excellent stead. I hope to be able to do as well, but I know it will be difficult.

Finally, I must mention computers and mobile phones. Yes, I realise how much you hate these, and cannot understand what we are doing spending so much time surfing the net and sending text messages. However, these are not just machines, but powerful means of improving world-wide communication,. We may have found new ways of talking to each other and writing to each other, but it is still communication, one of the most important things there is.

So you can see that I am really very optimistic. If we can avoid killing ourselves with nuclear weapons, or destroying the planet by pollution and environmental damage, there is a very exciting future for us all.

These thoughts came to my mind as I started to write to wish you a happy birthday. I hope it will make you happy to know how I am thinking and how you have helped me.

All my love

Your grandson

Jamie

- **Write a letter to the local newspaper explaining what you think should be done to prevent EITHER prejudice to different groups of people OR violence and disorderly behaviour on the streets.**

The Editor
Newtown Times

Dear Sir or Madam,

I am writing to you today because I am afraid, not for myself, but for what is happening to our community. The cause of my fear is the prejudice which I see all around me, prejudice which is making the lives of many individuals and groups unbearable, and which is threatening the very peace and stability of society.

I believe that a local newspaper can do a great deal to help stamp out such prejudice. I believe that we need a fundamental change in the way in which we regard those who, in one way or another, are not quite the same as us.

Above all, we need to understand how much prejudice there is, who its victims are and what the causes and effects are. This subject has been written about many times before and this letter is just a small contribution to the debate. However, there are a few points which need to be made. The first is that we must all believe in equal rights and opportunities for all people, regardless of their race, sex or abilities. It saddens me how many people still seem to think that they have some natural right to think of themselves as superior, because of the colour of their skin or their physical or mental abilities. Surely, in this multi-faith, multi-cultural society there is no place for intolerance? I know that some people are suspicious of the arrival of different ethnic groups in this country, claiming that they are destroying our society, or stealing our jobs and trying to impose their values on us. Yet in reality this country has always been a home to different people, right from ancient times. Our society owes much to the varied people who make up our country today. They have enriched our whole lives, our culture, attitudes and even the food we eat.

So I believe that your newspaper should support all minorities, recognising their achievements, celebrating their way of life and promoting harmony among everyone. I have concentrated on racial prejudice, because this is what is most often the cause of violence. But there are other important points I could have made if I had time. Women still earn less than men in many areas, have less good jobs and life chances, and are even viewed in a sexist way or as second-class citizens. Then there are our attitudes to those with physical 'disabilities'. We should recognise that many such people have abilities far greater than ours in some respects, and we should be continuing the campaign to give the widest possible access to facilities. For instance, is it not true that a survey of our streets and entertainment centres would show what a long way we still have to go to allow those confined to wheelchairs to take full advantage of life in our community?

With your help, we in Newtown can do much to create a more tolerant Britain. I urge you, and all your readers, to join with me in doing as much as we can to bring about a society which is more tolerant and is fair to all. Equal opportunities should be our goal, and we should admit that we have a long way to go to get there.

Yours sincerely

Francesca Wilson

Glossary of non-fiction terms

Argument – a series of points put together clearly to construct a clear case

Article – a piece of writing, on a particular topic, from a newspaper or magazine

Audience – the person or people being addressed by a speaker or writer

Autobiography – the story of someone's life (or part of that life), written by the actual person, sometimes with the help of a 'ghost-writer'

Biography – the story of someone's life (or part of that life), written by somebody else

Diary – a regular series of entries (e.g. daily) in a personal book which records one's experiences

Form – the kind and style of writing required for a particular purpose (e.g. article, letter, report)

Interview – a conversation (often on television or radio) between two people, with one (the interviewer) asking the questions of the other (the interviewee)

Journal – a more formal diary or record of daily proceedings, perhaps written for publication

Manual – a handbook, usually containing advice, information or instructions about an activity or product

Paragraph – a self-contained section of text, with a number of linked sentences contributing to a distinct set of ideas or information. The start of a paragraph is usually indicated, in a hand-written text, by beginning the first line slightly in from the left-hand margin

Report – an account of events, such as news items, or of an individual's or a group's ideas, delivered to an audience, e.g. a superior officer or the general public

Summary – a short version of a longer piece of writing (such as a book or article), giving only the main points.

media

Introduction

A range of media may be studied for this paper, as set down in the National Curriculum. Unseen materials for Papers 3 and 5 will be drawn from print-based media texts:

- advertisements
- brochures
- magazines
- leaflets
- newspapers
- mailshots.

You may be asked to work on one text or to compare one or more texts. Remember, you do not need to have followed a media studies course. The Glossary of media terms on page 81 will be helpful.

You should be able to take into consideration audience, purpose and style, both in commenting on texts and in producing your own texts in response to questions.

This section covers examples from some of the more common types of media source:

- newspaper articles
- advertisements
- leaflets
- mailshots

There are comments, points to consider and tasks for each source, as well as a further list of questions for you to work on (on page 74).

Newspaper sources

In your study of English, you will almost certainly have used newspapers on a number of occasions, perhaps for different purposes. You will have looked, perhaps, at the different types of newspapers, which are set out in the Glossary on page 81. There are many things to think about, for example:

- What is news?
- Are newspapers only about news?
- Can we believe what we read in them?
- Are they fair, or is there bias?
- How are stories presented?
- What part is played by photographs and other pictures?
- How do the layout and design of papers affect the reader?
- What are the main differences between tabloids and broadsheets?
- How do different sizes of print or use of different fonts influence the reader?
- What is the intended audience?

Newspapers can do a number of things:

- They can inform the reader.
- They can analyse events.
- They can try to persuade you.

These relate closely to the way in which you may be asked to respond to newspaper sources for Papers 3 and 5.

Responding to newspaper sources: an example

'Cyber Pets Will Escape Quarantine'
Carefully read the source set out opposite.

> *You should refer closely to the article when studying the topics below.*

The subject of 'quarantine' is one which has attracted a great deal of interest in recent years. It is a very controversial issue, and one on which many people feel strong emotions. There are several features of the way in which the article is written and set out which contribute to its effect. Think about the following features:

- headlines
- captions
- language
- use of individual cases and interviews
- illustrations
- graphics
- layout
- font size
- key words.

Are there other features which you think are important?

Using this list, consider carefully, by close reference to the article, the aims of the writer, and how the writer achieves these aims. How successful has the writer been? Discuss the extent to which the newspaper presents the issues about the subject fairly.

- Analyse the effectiveness of the presentation.
- Comment on the language and the argument.
- Look closely at the use of visual material.

You have now thought about the **content, design, purpose, effectiveness and language** of the article. There are other ways in which you may be able to think about this article and subject. For example, in the article, the writer invites further comment from readers, by:

- writing a letter;
- dictating a letter by phone.

Compose a letter to the newspaper in which you express your own opinions.

We are told that on, page 8 of the same newspaper, there is an **editorial** (see Glossary on page 81) on this subject. Look at the specimen question and the model answer on page 77.

> **Remember**, *on the Media paper, you will have one reading question (based on the content and how it is presented) and two writing questions, which use the text as a stimulus.*

Cyber pets will escape quarantine

Reunited

MICROCHIP TO ACT AS PASSPORT FOR ANIMALS

A REVOLUTIONARY microchip – no bigger than a grain of rice – is the key to ending the agony of quarantine for thousands of pet owners.

Under present anti-rabies regulations, dogs, cats and other pets have to be isolated in kennels for six months on arrival in Britain from abroad.

But under a new scheme to be unveiled by the Government this week, pets which have been vaccinated against rabies can be "tagged" with a special microchip and issued with their own "pet passport".

The chip is inserted in the pet's neck by syringe and checked with an electronic scanner similar to a supermarket checkout gun.

When an animal arrives in the country, it will be scanned. If the information on the chip matches the pet's papers, it can enter.

Distress

But animals being imported from countries where rabies is rife will still have to endure the solitary confinement.

News of the change – which is expected to become law next year – has been welcomed by pet owners.

Apart from the distress caused to their pets, they have campaigned against quarantine for three reasons:

COST: To keep their family pets in quarantine for six months, owners have to pay £1,387 for a dog and £1,279 for a cat.

The RSPCA estimate that the new system – which would involve buying an import licence, vaccination, blood testing and the microchip implant – would cost between £300 and £400 – a massive saving.

Sun SPECIAL REPORT

DEATHS: Three thousand animals have died in quaranting since 1975.

SMUGGLING: Customs officers are constantly catching people trying to bring pets into Britain illegally.

RSPCA official Alex Ross said: "We have been campaigning for this for some years. We believe vaccinating animals against disease is safer and just as effective as quarantine. And it is more humane."

Lady Mary Fretwell, who runs the campaign group Passports for Pets, said: "We very much welcome that the Government has finally grasped the nettle on this and hope there are no more delays. I have betrayed my dogs three times in 30 years by putting them in quarantine.

June Hamilton, of the Quarantine Abolition Fighting Fund, said: "I am delighted that at last we are getting some action. It was recommended to the Government in 1994 that the system should be scrapped. Since then we would estimate 80 to 100 animals have been smuggled into Britain every week."

Pressure

The scale of the problem is revealed by figures which show that last year 4,028 dogs, 3,351 cats, 692 chinchillas and 434 rabbits were among animals quarantined.

Among those who have suffered are the Fraser family of Kew, Surrey.

They visit their 18-month old cat Amy every Saturday afternoon in kennels at Willowslea Farm in Stanwell Moor, Surrey. Amy returned with the family two months ago from Vietnam where husband Paul worked in the construction industry for two years.

He and his wife Alicia and two daughters Roya, 11 and Taya, 8, are faced with making the trip every week for the next four months.

Alicia, 43, said: "It is terrible. The only day we can visit is Saturday because the children are in school. Amy is always very pleased to see us. She rubs herself against our legs and purrs. Six months is such a long time."

The Government decided last October to review the current quarantine arrangements after coming under mounting pressure from animal welfare groups and pet owners.

WHAT DO YOU THINK?

What do you think about the plan to scrap the quarantining of pets? Write to: PETS, The Sun, 1 Virginia St, London E1 9BW.

Advertisement sources

Advertising

Advertising is the use of techniques to sell products or services, by appealing to a reader, viewer or audience.

- People advertise through the use of different **media**, which include:

television	newspapers
cinema	magazines
radio	publicity leaflets
posters	mailshots.

- Advertising may seek to:

persuade	flatter
tempt	appeal to vanity or greed
excite	raise aspirations or expectations.

- Advertisements tend to:
  select information to suit a purpose;
  aim at a particular audience (targeting) by sex or age, or a particular social group or interest group.

- Advertisements rely heavily on:
  hard-hitting slogans or catchphrases
  jingles (tunes with words)
  unusual visual images
  unexpected ideas or new twists.

Charity advertising

In this section you can see examples of **charity advertisements**. These are a type of source-material frequently used as a stimulus in examination papers (Papers 3 and 5). Other types of advertising are shown in the sections on **leaflets** (page 64) and **mailshots** (page 68).

The two advertisements here were issued by 'Oxfam' and 'Help the Aged' in 1998, and some details have now changed.

Both are major charities which are well-known and have operated for a long time.

Both are asking for a response to the situations of people in developing countries.

One is a direct money-making appeal. The other is a competition, designed to raise awareness of social issues.

SHE HAS NOWHERE LEFT TO TURN.

PLEASE DON'T TURN THE PAGE

You could be Tsering's last hope. She has little or no food to eat, and lives in a tiny, insanitary mud shack. Without help soon she could die.

Yet by sponsoring an elderly person like Tsering for just £10 a month, you could provide the food, clothing and medicines they need to survive.

In return, you'll receive regular reports on your adopted grandparent. For more details, please complete the form below.

Yes, I'm interested in helping an elderly person overseas. Please send me details.

Mr / Mrs / Miss / Ms _____

Address _____

_____

_____ Tel. No. _____

Postcode _____

Return to:
Helen Higgs,
Adopt a Granny
Help the Aged
FREEPOST LON 13041
PO Box 203
London N1 9BR

Help the Aged

Adopt a Granny
Registered Charity No. 272786

We're looking for winning designs for a brand new range of mugs

- Your design can be any colour or shape as long as it looks good on a standard sized mug.
- Your slogan could be a word, a phrase, or a whole sentence as long as it sums up what *Fair Trade* means to you.

The prize

The winning design will be put on to mugs by workers in a *Fair Trade* ceramics factory in Thailand, and sold in Oxfam *Fair Trade* shops.

Each winner will receive

- a set of six mugs, presented in their local Oxfam shop
- £100 worth of development-education resources for their school.

The press will be there to see you collect your prize.

This is *Fair Trade*

All too often, the farmers who grow much of the food we buy in our supermarkets are paid barely enough to live on. Take bananas, for instance.

Felix Bernard, a banana farmer in the Windward Islands, is having a tough time. The price he gets for his crop at market has fallen drastically in the last few years. He and other farmers can't compete with powerful transnational companies which have driven many of the world's smaller producers out of business.

Farmers like Felix depend on bananas. They need a fair price for their crop, or they'll go out of business. A *Fair Trade* banana could be one way to secure the future prosperity of the islands. Oxfam is working with farmers to help them to produce high-quality bananas for the *Fair Trade* market.

Look our for these bananas in your supermarket. Buy them and you'll be *Fair Trading*.

How to enter

You can enter the competition in one of two age categories: 14-16 years or 16-18 years (sixth form). The winning designs will be used on mugs to be sold in Oxfam's *Fair Trade* shops.

Feel free to use any medium - paint, gouache, crayon, pastel, ink, or any other. Be innovative. You want your design to be head and shoulders above the rest.

Write your name, address, school and age clearly on the back of your entry and send it to: Liz Leaver, Oxfam Campaigns, 274 Banbury Road, Oxford OX2 7DZ.

Closing date: 30 November 1998

fast with Oxfam on 13 November 1998
Find out more. Call the fastline on 0990 084225

Oxfam's fast

Oxfam GB is a member of Oxfam International. Registered Charity No. 202918.   Code:103039   SC/152H/98

you'd be a mug to miss out

enter our exciting competition

Oxfam's fast
13 November 1998

SEE OVER FOR DETAILS ▶

Looking at advertisements

Although the examination will use printed advertisements, the use of different forms of advertising in preparation and coursework will certainly be helpful, to think more fully about advertisers' techniques.

People are generally most aware of television or radio advertisements. By thinking about these, you can identify the different ways in which advertisers try to work on people to make them buy a product. In the past, advertising often contained a 'hard sell', in which the listeners or viewers had the message about the product 'rammed down their throats'. Nowadays, advertisers more often go for subtler approaches, often so subtle that it is difficult to be sure what is being advertised or why a particular image or storyline is used.

- Analyse advertisements you know, from various sources, thinking about the selling techniques employed.

Some questions to discuss

- How much are you influenced by advertisements?
- Which *medium* of advertising (e.g. radio, magazines) do you find most effective, and why?
- Choose two advertisements, one which you find particularly effective and one which you do not. Analyse why. (Compare your choices with a friend, and discuss.)
- How do advertisers target the young? Does this have any desirable or undesirable effects?
- Advertisers are sometimes referred to as 'hidden persuaders'. Does this seem to you an appropriate term or not?

Comparing advertisements

Many examination questions ask for a comparison of two advertisements. If you compare the Oxfam and Help the Aged advertisements, you could look at, for example:

- immediate impact
- visual techniques
- use of captions or slogans
- content of text
- tone of language
- target audience
- action required.

> *Question 1* concentrates on content, language, layout and design.
> *Question 2* may ask you to adapt the content or form for a particular writing purpose: analyse, comment, review.

Leaflet sources

Publicity leaflets

Publicity leaflets may be issued for a variety of purposes. They may be a direct or indirect form of advertisement, but their common aim is to provide information about an organisation. To examine the effect of different forms of leaflet:

○ Make a collection of leaflets which you have obtained from a variety of sources. These may come from such places as: stations, libraries, tourist information offices, hotels.

○ See what different types you can collect, what range of services or products are covered, and what information they contain.

Leeds Castle

- Study the Leeds Castle leaflet carefully, noting down the information you learn from it, the selling-points which are stressed, and the way in which the pictures and text are used together.
- Look at the specimen questions on page 74 and the model answer on page 78.
- If you were going to answer the question about a new facility for Leeds Castle, what would your suggestion be?
- Choose one other castle or famous building known to you, and prepare a publicity leaflet to advertise it.
- If you have time, practise one or both of the specimen questions, giving yourself no more than 35-40 minutes, as in a GCSE examination.

A castle for all seasons.

LEEDS Castle, one of the most romantic and most ancient castles in the Kingdom. In the 9th century, this was the site of a manor of the Saxon royal family. Listed in the Domesday Book, this castle has been a Norman stronghold, a royal residence to six of England's mediaeval Queens, a playground and palace to Henry VIII and a private home.

Today, lovingly restored and now administered by the Leeds Castle Foundation, it is home to a magnificent collection of mediaeval furnishings, paintings, tapestries and treasures. This is a place where visitors of the present meet with lives of the past. You sense it, walking the grounds, where even the leaves breathe history.

HISTORIC PARK AND GARDENS.

The crowning glory of this most English of castles is its setting. On two small islands in the midst of an encircling lake, surrounded by a green arc of parkland, thick with trees and hills that tumble gently down to the water's edge. Within the 500 acre park, there are woodland walks, lakes and waterfalls, gardens and greenhouses. And so many glorious castle views, Kings and Queens and seasons may change, but Leeds Castle's enchanting and very English beauty is lasting, whatever the time of year.

ROYALTY AND ROMANCE.

The castle was first built in stone by Norman barons nearly 900 years ago to overawe the English. On Edward's I's accession, it was conveyed to the Crown, and for the next three centuries was a royal palace; fortified, enlarged, enriched and much loved by successive English Kings and Queens.

Love, romance and happiness have been in the air at Leeds Castle down the centuries; certainly for Queen Eleanor of Castile, Catherine de Valois and Henry VIII, the most celebrated of all the owners.

THE LEEDS CASTLE FOUNDATION FUNDING THE FUTURE.

A past that's not preserved soon becomes a past that is forgotten. Leeds Castle was saved for the nation when Lady Baillie, the last private owner, established the Leeds Castle Foundation on her death in 1974. The objectives of this independent charitable trust are to preserve the castle and park in perpetuity for the benefit and enjoyment of the public; to enable use of the castle for important national and international meetings, particularly for the advancement of medical research and for the furtherance of peace; and to promote artistic and cultural events.

Leeds Castle receives no major grants or government funding. The income raised from visitors, conferences, private functions and special events (including open-air concerts), is essential for the continued conservation of this important heritage site for future generations.

LEEDS CASTLE

Maidstone in Kent

ADY Baillie's purpose and ambition was to preserve Leeds not merely as history, but as 'a living castle.' Now adults and children of all ages, nationalities and interests, enjoy the great variety of things to see and do in the castle and park. Living testimony that the ambition is realised. To make the most of it all, allow around 3 to 4 hours for your visit.

THE CASTLE DEFENCES.

The Barbican, Fortified Mill and Gatehouse form part of the castle's concentric defence system, developed by Edward I in the 13th century. Revetment towers, arrow slits and murder holes are a reminder of Leeds original function – an impregnable fortress.

THE CASTLE AND TREASURES.

Richly furnished and decorated throughout with carved beams, Tudor stonework, fine wallhangings and Flemish tapestries – each room is teeming with treasures. You'll walk through history. From the Norman cellar to the mediaeval Gloriette, from Henry VIII's Banqueting Hall and the royal chapel, to the beautiful drawing rooms created in the 1930s. Their stories and secrets are brought alive for you by the castle guides in each room.

CULPEPER GARDEN.

Created in 1980 and named after the Culpeper family, 17th century owners of Leeds Castle. Like a cottage garden on a grand scale, it's a perfect setting for a delightfully informal collection of English flowers – roses, pinks, lad's love, lavender and lupins – many with wonderful scents. A herb border heightens the fragrance.

THE AVIARY.

This spectacular modern aviary was opened by H.R.H. Princess Alexandra, Royal Patron of the Leeds Castle Foundation, in 1988. It houses a collection of more than 100 rare species of bird, and aims not only at conservation, but also at successful breeding – to reintroduce endangered species into their original habitats.

WOOD GARDEN AND PAVILION GARDEN.

Conceived in the 1920s as a 'green garden', it is especially lovely in spring with its carpets of daffodils, narcissi and wood anemones bordering the meandering streams and small lakes. Later, azaleas and rhododendrons emblazon these gardens.

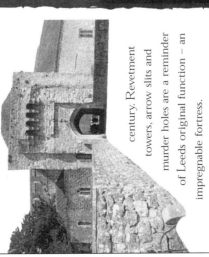

THE MAZE

Planted in 1987 with 2,400 yew trees. Children love getting lost in the maze and it's fun for grown-ups too. At the centre a viewing mound – a hollow dome – a grotto that takes you from the light of day into a fantastic underworld of beasts and legends, tunnels and tumbling water.

1998 SPECIAL EVENTS AND ENTERTAINMENTS.

✤ New Year's Day Treasure Trail – 1 Jan.

✤ A Celebration of Easter – 11 to 13 April.

✤ Festival of English Food & Wine – 16 & 17 May.

✤ Balloon & Vintage Car Fiesta – 6 & 7 June.

✤ Annual Open Air Concerts, Royal Liverpool Philharmonic Orchestra with the Band and Guns of the Royal Artillery – 27 Jun & 4 Jul (advance tickets only).

✤ Flower festival – 16 to 19 Sept.

✤ Grand Firework Spectacular – 7 Nov.

✤ Christmas Celebrations – decorations, floodlighting and carollers from mid-Dec. Christmas Shop from 1 Nov.

✤ Half-term Fun for Children activities during Kent school holidays.

✤ Kentish Evening Dinners many Saturdays throughout the year: (inc. tour of castle, five course meal, wine and entertainment) 7pm to 12.30am (by reservation).

For information 24 hours a day, call our Special Events Line on 0891 800656**

** Calls cost 39p per minute cheap rate and 49p per minute at all other times.

OPEN EVERY DAY (Except Christmas Day).

March to October Park & Gardens 10am to 5pm*. Castle 11am to 5.30pm*. (Ticket office closes 5pm).

November to February Park & Gardens 10am to 3pm*. Castle 10.15am to 3.30pm*. (Ticket office closes 3pm).

* Last admission. Park & Gardens close two hours after last admission.

(Closed 27th June, 4th July prior to Open Air Concerts.)

♿ Disabled visitors are especially welcome. Full details of accessibility and special facilities throughout the castle and grounds are given in a special leaflet available on request in advance, or on arrival. We regret no dogs except guide dogs and hearing dogs.

The trustees reserve the right to close all or part of the castle as necessary.

TOURS FROM LONDON.

Britainshrinkers – 01963 34616. Evan Evans Tours – 0181 332 2222. Frames Rickards – 0171 837 3111. Golden Tours – 0171 233 7030. Green Line – 01634 832666. Travellers Check-In – 0171 636 7175. Venice Simplon-Orient-Express – 0171 805 5100. For further details and bookings contact the company direct, your hotel porter or concierge, or a tourist information centre.

For information and news 24 hours a day, call – Leeds Castleline 0891 800680.**

Leeds Castle, Maidstone, Kent ME17 1PL

Tel: (01622) 765400. Fax: (01622) 735616

Internet http://www.se-eng-tourist-board.org.uk/seetb/(see places to visit).

The best day out in history.

THE DUCKERY.

Created in the 1960s out of a wilderness of tangled brambles and fallen trees, it is now the natural habitat for a fine collection of unusual and exotic waterfowl – pintail, mandarin and eider ducks, red-breasted Russian geese, black swans, even peacocks – which also roam free within the grounds.

DOG COLLAR MUSEUM.

Hunting dogs, gundogs, mastiffs to guard the castle gate, spaniels and lapdogs to grace the apartments of widowed Queens. Down the years, dogs have been part of life at Leeds Castle. So it is appropriate that here is the world's finest collection of antique dog collars, with examples ranging over 400 years.

FAIRFAX HALL AND TERRACE ROOM RESTAURANTS.

Snacks, salads, cream teas and a good variety of hot meals are available with a choice of

of self-service meals in the 17th century Fairfax Hall or a table service menu in the Terrace Room. fast food in the Stable Yard, self-service

Lovely gifts and souvenirs are available from shops, both nearby and at the park entrance – where there is also a parkland picnic site.

Mailshot sources and promotional literature

Sending mailshots

'Accident Protection Plan' is one of many companies which send out promotional envelopes to a large number of houses. These are often termed 'junk mail' – by those who receive them rather than those who send them.

The example below is from a recent mailing of a large pack of leaflets and letters in a thickly-packed envelope. Those who send out such mailshots are usually trying, directly or indirectly, to sell a product or service. If they were not, there would be no point in their doing it.

Many people who receive what they regard as 'junk mail' automatically throw it out without looking at it.

○ **Think about** how APP tries to stop you wanting to throw away their mailshot.

○ **Consider**:
layout
language
tone
selling-points

○ **Decide**:
at whom it is aimed;
whether you think it is effective;
how it might be improved.

Accident Protection Plan
APP House, 120-125 Dickens Mews, London WCC1 44XX

Mr A Brown
2 Fairmile Road
Paxton
London
W4 5SD

Tuesday 29th September 1998

Dear Mr Brown,

We are delighted to tell you that you have won a prize with Lucky Number 2845815 in our NEW £200,000 CASH DRAW.

What have you won? It may be the £25,000 TOP CASH AWARD. Or maybe one of FIVE £1,000 or TWENTY £300 Cash Wins, or one of 1,000 special Accident Protection Plan rollerball pens.

To claim your confirmed win, simply FILL IN THE SPECIAL FORM enclosed and post it in the reply-paid envelope to reach us by the closing date 31st October 1998. If you have won the top award of £25,000 you can double your money if you send the form back within seven days.

A Commissioner for Oaths has already drawn the winning numbers at random – and YOURS is one of them!

Before you fill in the form, we would like you to consider this offer of accident insurance. Imagine what would happen to a relative or friend, who suffered an injury and could never lead a normal life again. Everyone is at risk, driving, on the train or the bus, in an aeroplane, or even just crossing the road!

Suppose a victim of a sporting accident survived – but lost the use of his or her legs. Wouldn't receiving a CASH Lump Sum of £75,000 help them to come to terms with their disablement? The Accident Disablement Protection Plan costs less than 10 pence a day and gives you protection world wide. You can also have extra cover for special risks.

DON'T DELAY!! Take out an Accident Protection Plan Policy today. Don't forget, all you have to do is fill out the back of the form claiming your prize. We will do the rest.

Barclays Insurance leaflet

From the leaflet on this page and page 70, you can see that Barclays Bank is also trying to sell insurance. There is a single sheet, double-sided.

Notice the particular selling-points used: if Barclays wishes you to change from your existing company, you must be persuaded. The message is therefore a direct one. It stresses:

- value
- opportunity
- service
- additional features.

- Pick out the examples of how Barclays tries to tempt the reader. What would be most likely to encourage you to change to Barclays? Why might you decide not to?
- To whom is this leaflet trying to appeal? Is it successful?
- Compare the two approaches of the insurance companies. Which of these is more likely to attract you and to make you want to buy? Why?

Quality cover, guaranteed lower premiums. An offer that's too good to miss.

As a Barclays customer, not only can you now enjoy the benefits of quality car insurance, but we even guarantee to beat your current renewal premium. Our flexible car insurance can be arranged over the phone with the minimum of fuss and no lengthy form to fill out. As well as taking the hassle out of purchasing car insurance, our unique offer, combined with quality cover, guarantees you a great deal.

As well as excellent cover, you can expect far more for your money

From the moment you choose Barclays Car Insurance, you can expect a service which not only gives real value for money, but also offers a range of benefits you'll find hard to beat. What's more, you'll begin to enjoy the extra peace of mind which comes from knowing you

have dedicated professionals working on your behalf. After all, Barclays are one of the world's leading and most respected financial organisations.

With our tailor-made cover, we'll treat you as an individual

Your unique documentation is tailored to you, clearly explaining only the cover that you've asked for and making your policy simple and easy to understand.

Our comprehensive car insurance policy offers the following features:

1. We authorise all repairs fast

In the event of your vehicle requiring repair work, the last thing you'll want is any unnecessary delay. That's why, at Barclays, we use the latest video technology to authorise repairs swiftly and efficiently. And you'll have access to our 24 hour accident recovery line, 365 days of the year. Add to this the fact that our repair network incorporates only the very best repair specialists, and you can rely on expert assistance,

when you need it most. And all repairs are fully guaranteed for 3 years.

2. A courtesy car, absolutely free

Should you need to make a claim, we'll do everything we can to make things easier for you. For instance, we'll provide a courtesy car totally free of charge for the duration of the repairs (providing your vehicle is being repaired by a Barclays approved repairer). And that's not all, your repaired car will be cleaned inside and out before it's returned to you.

3. Replacement cover for all audio equipment

Subject to a reasonable excess, our unlimited audio equipment cover means that in the event of theft or damage, you have the peace of mind

of having everything fully covered, and that we can normally replace the equipment within a few days.

Please note that in order to take advantage of our guarantee you will need to:

1. Pay your premium in one payment by Connect Card, Barclaycard or by most other debit or credit cards.

2. Provide proof of your renewal premium.

To save time when you call, please remember to have your renewal documents to hand.

N.B. This guarantee cannot apply to renewal premiums issued by Barclays Car Insurance.

Offer expires 30th July 1999

We are not able to provide quotes for:

- Motorcycles
- Commercial vehicles
- Cars used for business only

Call now on 0870 600 1414 quoting ref 9813 or fill in the coupon

And remember, if you require cover to commence within the next 30 days, please telephone us immediately on the number provided. Lines open 8am–9pm weekdays, 9am–Saturday 5pm.

Analyse, review, comment: pointers for Question 2

As was mentioned on page 50, the GCSE syllabus sets out a number of ways of writing which are assessed in different parts of the syllabus and examination.

- ○ Question 2 on papers 3 and 5 is designed to test candidates' ability to write according to the **Range of Writing: Analyse, Review, Comment**.
- ○ The main assessment objective is **to adapt writing for particular purposes and audiences.**
- ○ The supporting assessment objectives are to:

  organise ideas into sentences and paragraphs;
  use grammatical structures of Standard English;
  use a wide vocabulary;
  express meanings with clarity and precision.

You will need to read the question carefully to see how it relates to one or more of the three words 'analyse', 'review' and 'comment'. The question will be based closely on the media text or texts provided for the examination, which will have been studied for Question 1. (In question 1 candidates write on the content of the texts, being assessed for reading.) For question 2, candidates will be assessed on their ability to **write in a particular way**, related to the range of writing mentioned above: the form might be a letter, or report, for example.

Analyse

Analysis is a term used in different subjects of the curriculum. In English, analysis usually consists of the close examination of texts, studying, for example:

- ○ their form;
- ○ their language;
- ○ their structure;
- ○ their purposes.

Analysis is often the first part of a process: after breaking something down into its parts, we usually need to put it together again, now that we can see how it works: this is the process of synthesis.

- • Ask yourself questions about the different ways of analysing text:

  Form   - the kind of text; the design of the text;
  Language - straightforward? ornate? factual? ironic? direct? subtle?
  Structure - simple or complex?
  Purposes - inform, explain or describe?
             - analyse, review, comment?
             - argue, persuade, instruct?

Review

To review something is, at its simplest, to 'look at it again'. The most common kind of review with which you are likely to be familiar in English is the book review, where you may be asked to:

- ○ give your response;
- ○ explain your reasons;
- ○ offer an opinion;
- ○ make a recommendation.

For Question 2, you may be asked, as part of your response, to:
- review the evidence and decide what it tells you;
- review different approaches and judge their suitability or effectiveness;
- review advantages and disadvantages and come to a conclusion or recommend a solution.

You should be aware that the process of **review** will also require close **analysis** and involve making **comment**.

Comment

We comment on people or objects for various reasons and in different ways, but mainly to express our opinion of them. The same is true when commenting on texts or arguments. It is important to think about the reasons why we comment and the kinds of comment we make. These may be to express:
- approval
- amusement
- delight
- praise
- admiration
- disgust
- relief.

In an English response, much more is needed. You may need to comment on:
- **what** your reactions or views are;
- **why** you feel or think as you do;
- **how** you think someone should act.

Comment, therefore, must be **clear** and **personal**, but also **well-argued** and **fully-supported**.

NB Whether the writing is **analysing**, **reviewing** or **commenting**, or all three, it is important for it to be in the appropriate style.

Remember the main assessment objective!

Argue, persuade, instruct: pointers for Question 3

- Question 3 on papers 3 and 5 is designed to test candidates' ability to write according to the **range of writing : argue, persuade, instruct.**
- The main assessment objective is **to adapt writing for particular purposes and audiences.**
- The supporting assessment objectives are to:
  organise ideas into sentences and paragraphs
  use grammatical structures of Standard English
  use a wide vocabulary
  express meanings with clarity and precision.

You will need to read the question carefully to see how it relates to one or more of the three words, 'argue', 'persuade' and 'instruct'.
- **Argue:** You will be expected to develop a case or point of view; sometimes the question will ask you to present *both sides* of an argument and weigh up the strengths and weaknesses of each, coming to a conclusion.

○ **Persuade:** You will need to *convince* a reader or audience of what you are saying: you may wish to persuade someone of your view, or to change their mind, or to join a political party or campaign.

○ **Instruct:** Your task will be to *teach* someone how to do something, or give them *orders* or *instructions* on what to do.

For this question, candidates may be asked to consider points from the stimulus material used in question 1 or to choose their own context for writing of this kind.

Argue

An argument should be clear, well-constructed and logical. The steps should follow as in a mathematical proof.

The word *therefore* (so, thus, hence, consequently) concludes an argument. Other connecting words help to develop it, such as:

○ and/but/for
○ moreover/however/because
○ also/nevertheless/since

Arguments should be: factual, objective, clear and unemotional

Persuade

How do you persuade someone?

○ Be confident;
○ Be convinced;
○ Be convincing;
○ Be conclusive;

○ Use a range of effective techniques;
○ Think of what persuades *you*;
○ Think of skilled persuaders.

A good persuader uses **rhetorical devices** (the tricks of public speakers) such as:

○ rhetorical questions;
○ exclamations;

○ direct appeals to the reader or listener;
○ colourful images and soundbites.

Instruct

This section is set out as a simple set of instructions:

You must speak or write in such a way that:

○ someone can follow a set of procedures;
○ you pass on your skills by clear explanations;
○ you make sure that what needs to be done is done;
○ the audience learns or understands the new knowledge required.

You should:

○ take things step by step, in a clear, simple structure;
○ give commands ('Do this…') or prohibitions ('Avoid this…') which are firm and direct;
○ check understanding at key stages.

Do not:

○ make things too complicated;
○ lose the thread;
○ write long sentences.

Non-fiction specimen questions: Questions 1, 2 and 3

The questions for Question 1 and Question 2 are to be answered with reference to media sources such as those earlier in the chapter. Some of the questions refer directly to the sources given on these pages, but you may choose other examples of your own choice on which to base your response. Question 2 on Papers 3 & 5 is designed to test candidates' ability to write according to the range of writing: analyse, review, comment.

Questions 1 & 2

Newspapers

Q 1   Study two articles, one from a broadsheet and one from a tabloid (or from different tabloids), which are written on the same subject. Summarise clearly the information and feelings conveyed by each, and show how the layout, presentation and language of each of these contribute to their effect.

Q 2   Write a newspaper 'leader' or editorial based on the issues raised in one of the articles.

Advertisements

Q 1   What are the ways in which each of these advertisements seeks to appeal to the reader? (Consider all relevant considerations of language, content and design.) Comment on the target audience at which you think that the advertisers are aiming.

Q 2   Write the report which you will present at your School Council, which puts forward three methods by which you intend to advertise the chosen school charity. Think about audience, style and use of media.

Leaflets

Q 1   Study carefully the attached publicity leaflet (pages 65–7). What does this tell you about the attractions of Leeds Castle and its suitability for a family day out? How clear do you find the layout and why?

Q 2   Write a letter to the managing director of the Leeds Castle foundation in which you set out your ideas for developing the site. You should analyse the possibilities offered by the buildings and grounds and comment on the advantages which your proposal will bring.

Mailshots and promotional literature

Q 1   You have obtained two types of promotional literature on the subject of insurance (see pages 68–70). Compare the effectiveness of the two approaches to promotion in making you want (a) to read them, and (b) to take the desired action.

Q 2   Imagine that you are an advertising executive, working for a mailshot company which is about to launch a new campaign. Put forward your proposals for a mailshot which will persuade people to take out insurance.

Question 3

Question 3 on papers 3 and 5 is designed to test candidates' ability to write according to the range of writing: Argue, Persuade, Instruct.

Q 1   Write a letter to the leader of your local Council, Ms Brown. In this, you should try to persuade the council not to grant permission for the building of another out-of-town supermarket which you believe will ruin the shops in the High Street.

Q 2   For a school Open Day, you have been asked to organise eight Year 11 (sixteen year-old) pupils to escort a group of prospective parents on a tour of the school. Write a sheet of clear instructions which will enable them to perform this task well.

Model answers: Question 1

- **What are the ways in which each of these advertisements seeks to appeal to the reader? (Consider all relevant considerations of language, content and design.) Comment on the target audience at which you think that the advertisers are aiming.**

These two advertisements feature two of Britain's best-known charities. 'Help the Aged' and 'Oxfam' are known for their campaigns of trying to bring aid to those in desperate need, and their names are familiar to large numbers of people.

These charities often appeal for financial help, and probably on seeing the name 'Oxfam' many people will immediately think that this is just another appeal for money. But when you look at the advertisement closely, it is clear that this is a different kind of appeal. It is, in fact, more of an invitation, or challenge. No money is asked for, and there is not even an entry fee for the competition which is advertised. If you are successful in the competition entry, you will even win £100 and a set of mugs, as well as the honour of having your design placed on mugs and sold in Oxfam's 'Fair Trade' shops.

Oxfam is aiming at something different from a straightforward money-raising appeal. To find out what that is, it is necessary to read the text closely — which the intriguing picture encourages you to want to do. The answer eventually comes in the explanation of the idea of 'Fair Trade', with the message emphasised by the example of a banana farmer from the Caribbean, Felix Bernard. Oxfam is deliberately putting across a message that it is not simply trying to raise money. It is trying to help the trade and industry in less developed countries, so that they will be able to survive. By supporting the bananas which are produced by small farmers such as Mr Bernard, Oxfam is drawing attention to the difficulties which recent trends have created: 'Farmers can't compete with powerful transnational companies which have driven many of the world's smaller producers out of business.' It is a campaign aimed at changing our buying habits. We must, it seems, become sensitive to the economic hardships faced by many developing countries which supply us with our fresh fruit and vegetables. Oxfam is undertaking to place on the shelves of supermarkets products with the 'Fair Trade' label, so that we can support the cause not by donating money directly but by buying their goods. The competition is designed to start to make its audience more aware of the name 'Fair Trade' and what it stands for. It is appealing to our sense of justice and fair play: 'Buy them and you'll be <u>Fair Trading</u>.'

The 'Help the Aged' advertisement is a more direct appeal for money: 'Please don't turn the page'. The picture of a desperately hungry old woman from a Third World country, with the specific country not actually mentioned, is a well-used approach. 'Help the Aged' is not promoting some complicated social or economic policy. It is simply saying that £10 a month will keep someone such as Tsering alive. There is, however, an additional touch: the 'Adopt a Granny' approach. In recent years, charities have increasingly used this technique to make donors feel a greater sense of personal involvement in the charity. The same approach has frequently been used for children and animals.

The difference in approach is underlined visually. Oxfam's style is punchy, humorous, up-to-date. There are clear typefaces and an arresting picture, the man with a banana mouth, which arouses curiosity and makes complete sense only after reading the text on the reverse. 'Help the Aged', on the other hand, has a traditional appearance, a stark black and white photograph and a short, straightforward message. It is not necessary to do too much thinking: simply fill in a form and find out more.

The appeal of the Oxfam advertisement is very clearly aimed at school pupils, especially those aged from 14 to 18, and their parents or teachers. The 'Help the Aged' appeal is more general. No specific age-group is specified, although it might be thought that the reference to adopting a 'granny' would be aimed at those who were fairly young.

The principal difference between the two seems to relate to the amount of effort required to respond to the appeal. One plainly needs more reading, more thought, a subtle appreciation of the charity's tactics. It is necessary to go away and do something: create a design and think about a slogan. The other simply requires the filling in of a form. Not even a stamp is needed, since the address is FREEPOST. The difference between the two is really the contrast between a simple fund-raising appeal and an approach which aims to make the young reader think about world social and economic issues.

- **You have obtained two types of promotional literature on the subject of insurance (see pages 68–70). Compare the effectiveness of the two mailshots in making you want (a) to read them, and (b) to take the desired action.**

The APP accident insurance mailshot and the Barclays Insurance leaflet picked up in the bank are two examples of persuasive literature which are an increasingly common feature of modern life: the attempt to sell something, often either a product or a financial service. These two examples are also both concerned with insurance, and they are dealing with important aspects of life: sickness and health and car insurance.

There are also, however, important differences in the techniques of selling, the type of appeal, the layout and the design. The 'APP' medical insurance letter is said to be part of a larger pack which arrived through the door in a thick, packed envelope. The Barclays leaflet, directed primarily at Barclays customers, is designed to stand alone. 'APP' has several items, all of which are designed to reinforce the basic messages, with considerable repetition. The promoters of APP rely on people's curiosity to open an important envelope; Barclays hope customers will be attracted by the quality of the design of their leaflet.

The difference in visual layout of the information is striking. The APP pack starts with a letter, which is always 'personalised' to a named addressee – a common device made possible by new computer techniques. The actual appearance of the letter is of interest. It is clearly meant to look as though it has been produced on an ancient, battered typewriter. There is a great deal of 'typed' text on the page.

The Barclays leaflet is quite different. There is a large-type caption, which has a clear message: 'Whatever your renewal premium, we will beat it'. The subject-matter is insurance, and the emphasis is on <u>quality</u> and <u>price</u>. The text is clearly set-out, using modern design techniques; it looks professionally designed, with text and pictures strategically arranged.

In both cases, the object of the mailing is to attract someone to buy insurance, but in the case of 'APP' that message is decidedly more hidden. This may be because those selling medical insurance feel that they have to do more to get people interested. Barclays know that what they have to do is try to increase their own share of the car insurance market, by offering a deal which will tempt someone to transfer from their existing policy. Their sales pitch is therefore based on offering lower prices, quality, service and additional features. The advertisement stresses in particular what good value for money the Barclays deal is, and everyone wants value for money.

In the APP mailshot, the text trades on the fact that many people do not have medical insurance, and may not initially be interested. So the leaflet starts not by talking about insurance at all, but about the chance to win some money. It appeals therefore to the most basic 'something for nothing' instinct. The 'cash win' is mentioned in the very first sentence of the letter.

'APP' also plays on our fear that anyone can suddenly be struck by a disabling illness, and it tries to bring home to the reader just what a dreadful experience that can be without insurance. This mailshot is therefore not trying to persuade people to transfer from one form of medical insurance to another, but to take out private insurance for the first time, because of increasing concerns about health care.

Cash prizes are meant to 'hook' readers, so that they are more likely to stay with the scheme than leave it. Barclays, however, is using its 'name', as one of the largest international banks, to persuade customers who value its services to extend their loyalty. The effectiveness of 'APP' may well depend on how tempted the readers are by cash prizes. Some may feel that the chances of winning one of the large cash prizes are very slight. However, there will be others who are tempted. The Barclays scheme will attract those who want the cheapest car insurance, supplied by a successful bank. A 'guaranteed' low price is more tempting than the offer of a cash prize — probably a very small one!

Model answers: Question 2

- **Write a newspaper 'leader' or editorial based on the issues raised in the article (page 59).**

It's a dog's life... ... or death. And it could be a human's life. Or death.

That's why quarantine is a topic which arouses such fierce emotions. Since 1975, three thousand animals have died in quarantine, like Julie's English setter. And how many more are there like Anna's Jack Russell, put down by their owners rather than being allowed to go through the long and lonely months of quarantine?

But that is just one side of the argument. The other is that the risk to human life of <u>not</u> having quarantine is so serious that it is worth even such a heavy death toll of animals. After all, this country, unlike many others, has been free from rabies for a very long time.

This is why the story which we are carrying today matters so much. For the first time ever, thanks to the wonders of modern technology, we now have a real chance to end quarantine without opening the floodgates to a fresh invasion of devastating disease.

We say that the time is ripe for a change. Thanks to new vaccines and the latest silicon advances, a nightmare for pets and owners can be ended once and for all. The pets' passport scheme is a winner. It is safe and it is sensible.

The Government should introduce it, and do so as soon as possible.

We know from our readers all over the country that there is a long list of tragic tales and personal hardship. Many ordinary people, whose pets are just like members of the family to them, and who provide them with love and devotion, are daily affected by rules which we shall soon be able to tear up. These people will give a loud cheer to a government which has the courage to open up the cages and let out these long-suffering pets, provided they are in good health, so that they can be reunited at long last with their owners.

We say: these animals have suffered enough.

So have their owners.

Now is the time to end this example of man's inhumanity to man's best friend.

● **Write a letter to the managing director of the Leeds Castle foundation in which you set out your ideas for developing the site. You should analyse the possibilities offered by the buildings and grounds and comment on the advantages which your proposal will bring.**

1 Main Street
Hightown, Kent

The Managing Director
The Leeds Castle Foundation

Dear Sir

I have recently seen a copy of your leaflet, advertising 'The best day out in history'. It is an excellent leaflet, and the range of facilities is very impressive. I have spent a day with my family at Leeds Castle, and there is a great deal to do which is most interesting, such as the unusual 'Dog Collar Museum' and the complicated and baffling maze.

I believe that I can suggest something which will make even more of your superb site and facilities, and would like to put forward some suggestions.

It seems to me that you have the opportunity to make much more of the <u>educational</u> possibilities of Leeds Castle, while still preserving its appeal as an entertaining day out. Your leaflet stresses the castle's <u>history</u>, and you refer to the connections with 'Royalty and Romance', which Henry VIII represents particularly well. The displays about Henry and other royal figures are very well-designed.

It is this <u>historical</u> link which I think you can make more of. Henry VIII is the ideal figure to enable you to develop the site so that children from all over Kent and beyond will be drawn to Leeds Castle.

Now I know you might say 'The last thing we need is hordes of rowdy children tramping all over our castle and its beautiful grounds', but I hope you will listen to my ideas. School groups will be offered activities to stimulate them so that all pupils will be fascinated and fully occupied. The teachers themselves will love it, because the content of these sessions will really teach history in an unforgettable way. There will be trained instructors employed by the castle to help organise the visiting groups.

My proposal is called: 'Step into History, with Henry VIII and his six wives'. Pupils will go on an imaginative 'trail' through the site, exploring the variety of the castle's buildings and landscape. The latest museum technology, for example, will employ a wide range of computer-based activities, featuring historical objects for the children to feel and explore, and using high-class animations and models. There will be actors in costume, representing Henry and his wives. These actors know all about the history and life of their characters, so that they are able to act out scenes from history and answer even the hardest questions which the children will ask. Children will be able to ride across the lake in a boat which is a copy of a sixteenth century barge. In the gardens, near the grotto and maze, they will be able to watch Henry himself, trying to persuade the Pope to let him divorce Catherine of Aragon and marry Anne Boleyn, followed swiftly by a scene of Anne preparing for her execution on Tower Green.

These are just a few of my ideas. I am sure I can help Leeds Castle to live up to the proud boast of its slogan: 'The best day out in HISTORY'.

Yours sincerely

Robert Page

Model answers: Question 3

- **Write a letter to the leader of your local Council, Ms Brown. In this, you should try to persuade the council not to grant permission for the building of another out-of-town supermarket which you believe will ruin the shops in the High Street.**

Range of writing: **argue, persuade, instruct**

Rose Cottage
Oak Drive
Newtown
Middleshire

Dear Ms Brown,

This week, four more shops in our historic High Street have become empty. Soon, unless you take drastic steps, the High Street will become a wilderness, with nothing but banks, building societies and estate agents. Surely you must see the dangers! Can we not put a stop to the growth of out-of town monstrosities, which are draining away the life-blood of our town?

Action has to be taken now! For too many years, the Council has allowed the widespread destruction of the many small businesses which once made our town a varied and pleasant place to shop. Planning consents have been tossed out like confetti. The green-field sites on which superstores have been built have become a jungle of brick and concrete, while the derelict shops stand deserted, an eyesore to the dwindling numbers of loyal shoppers who struggle to keep our town centre alive.

The solution is obvious: no more supermarkets. The time has come to say 'No!'. It is high time that our Council made some hard decisions. Indeed, the moment is long overdue.

I ask you to think very seriously about this subject. Five years ago, within the space of 100 yards, my route along the High Street took me past a number of excellent retail outlets. I will now mention just a few.

A sewing shop used to exist which stocked everything from fine embroidery silks to odd buttons. Now I shall scour the streets in vain for these valuable items — and, of course, they are nowhere to be seen on the countless rows of supermarket shelves. In each store everything looks the same, whereas the old sewing shop had real character and variety.

A bakery provided high-quality early morning fresh rolls and croissants, as well as a wonderful selection of patisserie, not to mention old-fashioned English cakes and puddings. When will the younger generation have the opportunity to taste such delights?

I used to walk past a remarkable hardware shop, catering not only for the needs of the DIY enthusiast, but crammed with those indispensable items for helping with any domestic crisis. An enquiry for such things at the new DIY superstore is met, alas, only with a blank stare. Supermarkets do not give us that old-fashioned service that people still look for.

Now, of course, all of these interesting and valuable shops have gone. And these I have mentioned are only the tip of the iceberg. So change your minds before it is too late, especially for the hundreds of non-driving local residents who cannot reach the huge car-park-dominated supermarkets. Change your minds and policies before the town which you claim to serve becomes a hollow shell, rather than a living, bustling community.

Yours sincerely,

Elizabeth Granville (Mrs)

- **For a school Open Day, you have been asked to organise eight Year 11 (sixteen year-old) pupils to take a group of prospective parents on a tour of the school. Write a sheet of clear instructions which will enable them to perform this task well.**

INTRODUCTION

Remember that you have been specially selected for this important task, and that the school is relying on you. The job itself is basically a straightforward one. You are responsible for a group of ten parents. You must meet them, escort them and deliver them at the right place and at the right time, and you must keep to the precise course that you have planned, with no deviation. All parents MUST end up at the school canteen at 1600 hours (four o'clock) exactly, for tea with the Head of Year 7 and the Year 7 Form Tutors.

PLAN YOUR ROUTE
- Decide where you are going. The route should have <u>eight</u> points on it, chosen to show what the school has to offer.
- Draw out the planned route, showing each of the stopping-places and the expected time of arrival at each.
- Check your route carefully with all the other seven groups, to avoid the risk of congestion at any one point.
- Ensure that there is a five-minute interval, at least, between one group's departure and the next group's arrival at the most popular venues, such as the computer room. It is potentially disastrous if one group is trying to leave a room while another is trying to enter it.

KNOW YOUR SCHOOL

You need to be very well-informed about the school. Spend some time studying the relevant school documents, especially the Brochure which goes to all prospective parents, which your group will have with them. Be knowledgeable and be informative.

SPEAK TO PARENTS

It is absolutely essential that you give a good impression to the prospective parents, by your words and manner. We would like to encourage them to send their children to this school, not frighten them off! Answer their questions clearly, simply and with a smile. They may ask you about details of school policy which are beyond you. Invite them to raise these questions with the staff who will be available to deal with their queries over tea, or write in to the head-teacher.

ENJOY THE EXPERIENCE

Above all, I hope that you will find this a thoroughly enjoyable opportunity to show many different aspects of the school to our visitors, to talk sincerely and interestingly about your own experiences (but, please, not too many gory details!), and answer what will certainly be some fascinating questions. Have a really good time and remember: be prepared, be efficient and be friendly.

Glossary of media terms

Advertisements

Billboard – a board with posters or advertisements displayed

Brochures – small booklets with glossy advertising

Junk mail – post which is sent unasked by companies trying to promote or sell products

Leaflets – small, often folded sheets of paper carrying information or publicity material

Mailshots – the circulation of a leaflet, letter or advertisement

Poster – a large notice or advertisement displayed publicly, e.g. on billboards, often with a strong visual interest

Small ads – short advertisements in magazines or newspapers

Magazines

General – magazines for a wide readership, not on specialist topics

Specialist – magazines on a particular subject such as a sport or cars

Media Terms

Bias – showing favour to one side; directing or slanting material for a specific purpose

Caption – a headline or a few words or phrases accompanying text or a picture

Editorial/leader – a leading article in a newspaper or magazine, summing up on a main subject covered

Feature articles – articles in a newspaper or magazine which deal, often at some length, with a particular topic

Fonts – different type styles, e.g. italic

Graphics – use of visual effects, especially generated by computer

Headline – a bold heading to an article in a newspaper or magazine, summing up the subject

News articles – articles in a newspaper or magazine which tell the story of current news events, e.g. wars

Punning titles – titles with puns, which are often used in headlines or sub-headings to catch the reader's attention

Soundbites – short, snappy phrases or statements meant to be remembered easily

Sub-heading – a smaller heading than a headline, used in the body of an article to divide sections of the text

Types of Newspaper

Broadsheet – a large-page 'quality' newspaper, e.g. *The Times*

Local evening – a paper issued in the afternoon to serve a particular locality, e.g. *London Evening Standard*

National daily – an everyday newspaper, either tabloid or broadsheet, covering the country

Regional daily – an everyday newspaper, issued for a specific area, e.g. *Birmingham Post*

Sunday – a weekly paper, issued only on Sunday, e.g. *The Observer*

Tabloid – a small-sized newspaper, aiming for mass circulation, e.g. *Daily Mirror*

examination answers
together with examiners' comments

This final section of the book contains answers in both official examinations and in trials for the new syllabus requirements from *Tracks 2*. These are reproduced just as they appeared, **including any spelling, punctuation or grammar errors**. (These are generally underlined in the text.) The 'examiners' comments' show how the different answers fit the descriptions given for the various grades and offer some suggestions for how to improved the standard.

Paper 2F: Twentieth Century Poetry and Non-Fiction (pre-released material)

The Foundation Tier Papers (2F and 3F) have a grade-range from C to G.

Question 1   (25 marks for Reading)

- Look again at the poem 'Old Man, Old Man' by U A Fanthorpe (page 27 in Tracks 2). Explain how the old man's life is different now from when he was younger. Give examples of how the writer's use of language shows the way he has changed.

Main assessment objective: develop and sustain interpretations of text

Candidate's response

In the poem Old Man, Old Man she <u>rites</u> as if she's a <u>freind</u> of the old man but she makes fun of him <u>aswell</u>. She says he <u>use</u> to be a very handy sort of man because she says he 'did it himself'. She says he was good with tools. His wife is now <u>probaly</u> dead because he has to do his own washing up now, he also had children but he doesn't seem very close to them, they don't come and visit him. It says he <u>was'nt</u> any good with his daughters.

Now he is very old he <u>cant</u> see very well. When he sees the old <u>women</u> she is like a cloud_meaning she is not very clear. She says she will find his hammer which it said <u>earlyer</u> on he lost. I think he was still trying to do things himself a bit but he <u>couldnt</u> even find his tools but when he was younger everything was in its right place and he was like an expert at doing things, now <u>hes</u> not.

He is getting very confused because he <u>cant</u> see very well and he <u>cant</u> find his way. He say_he <u>cant</u> get 'from Holborn to <u>Dury</u> Lane', which are places in London where he lived. He used to get cross with the television and tell jokes, but he doesn't tell them <u>anymore</u>. He is <u>loosing</u> his memory, he <u>cant</u> even remember <u>wether</u> <u>hes</u> had his <u>cigarrette</u>.

He <u>probly</u> spent too much time in his shed, doing jobs_not in the house with the family_he seems to be very <u>lonley</u> even before he was an old man. He hates being useless, but I think U A Fanthorpe likes him. He was good at doing things but now he <u>cant</u> do them and he has nobody left to be cross with.

In marking this question, examiners were looking for a focus on:
- ○ aspects of characterisation of the old man
- ○ appreciation and interpretation of the changes that had happened in his life
- ○ examples of Fanthorpe's language to illustrate these aspects.

Examiner's comments

- Language points are mentioned in a few places, but **need to be more fully developed to improve the grade**.
- In places examples are used, but at other times the comment is rather general. **More direct quotations would make a big difference.**
- Overall, a reasonably sound understanding of the old man's character is given, and there is some grasp of the way in which his life has changed. Further development would help.
- There is some insecurity technically. **Spelling errors and omission of punctuation marks**, such as the apostrophe in contractions, would need to be addressed to raise the standard.
- There are occasional signs of **personal response** but **not much analysis** is offered.
  GRADE AWARDED FOR THIS QUESTION: GRADE F

Question 2 (25 marks for Reading)

- **Look again at the prologue from *Notes from a Small Island* by Bill Bryson (pages 34 and 35 in *Tracks 2*). What impression does this give you of the town of Dover, at which Bill Bryson arrived?**
  Support your answer by detailed reference to the text.

Main assessment objective: read with insight and engagement

Candidate's response

Bill Bryson did not seem to like England much when he first arrived, perhaps this was because it was very foggy and late at night and places do not look their best then. However he did enjoy walking round the streets by him self, he felt that he had the town 'all to myself'. He seemed to quite like Dover at this time, but not so much later on.

He was abit worried because he was tired and needed somewhere to sleep. Unfortunatley all the places seemed to be shut up so he couldn't find any where to stay and he had missed the last train to London.

It was funny when he fell over the doorstep and sent all the milk bottles all over the place and was shouted at by a lady from up above. This made me want to find out more about what happened to him. I thought it was good too where he said about his French meal which sounds absolutly discusting.

He found a sort of shelter to try to sleep, but he didn't think this was very comfy as it had lots of bits sticking out and it got very cold. I don't think he realy liked Dover much at the middle of the night. But he did describe it very well, in the early morning. He wrote about the gulls and boats and it gave a good impresion of what it must of been like.

He found the people of Dover rather strange for example the man he met with the funny little dog that wanted to pee all the time, he wrote that he was always talking about the wether, which he thinks is not very nice in England.

He thinks Dover is a funny little place with some rather strange people and he cant find any where to sleep but it is quite a pretty town with a good hotel, eventhough he can't aford to stay there.

In marking this question, examiners were looking for a focus on:

- the capacity to evaluate the evidence provided about Bill Bryson's view of Dover;

    ○ the ability to read text thoughtfully and use descriptions aptly to develop the response;

    ○ the use of evidence from the text to support the argument.

Examiner's comments

- A number of relevant points are made.
- There is some evidence of engagement and fair understanding, but the writing is not always clear .
- The candidate should **make more use of the evidence** and **quote more fully** to improve the grade.
- There are some significant weaknesses in **spelling and punctuation**.
- The answer loses focus slightly in Paragraph 3. It is necessary to plan carefully and keep to the question.

GRADE AWARDED FOR THIS QUESTION: GRADE E

Question 3   *(25 marks for Writing)*

Range of Writing: **inform, explain, describe**

- **Look back to when you started a new school (infant, junior or secondary school, for example). Write an account of the events which took place and describe clearly your feelings about them.**

Main assessment objective: use and adapt form for specific purpose

Candidate's response

Four years ago I came to the high school. I remember exactly how I felt, I was extremely excited because I was starting a new school. I was looking forward to meeting new pupils, having a different teacher for every subject and trying for all the different sports teams. I was not worried at all about going into a slightly bigger school and being at the bottom again, this excited me. I already knew some of those who were joining the school.

I was so excited about the new term and new school, that when I bought my new school uniform, I tried it on at home straight away! My best friend from my primary school kept telling me that it is not exciting at all and that it is just as boring as primary school. I told her <u>different</u> and carried on looking forward to the end of the holidays.

The summer holidays were gradually coming to an end and I was so anxious to start school. I remember my first day very well. I got dressed and ready to go in good time and my friend Marie and her mum came and picked me up. When we arrived, I had a huge smile on my face. It took us a while to find our classroom but we found it okay in the end. I recognised a lot of people from the day when we had visited the school at the end of the summer term. Our teacher soon came in and sat us in our places, I was sat next to a boy who was a complete stranger to me. As the day proceeded, I kept the smile on my face and I loved the first day in secondary school! It was a school with all sorts of new challenges.

As the year went on and I was finally settled in, my enthusiasm for coming to the big school died down a little, I was of course still very pleased to be there but I began to realise that it just another school with more work and longer hours. During the first three or four weeks, I was still getting lost but managed <u>to always</u> find my way to the classes. In my first year, Mr Johnson always taught French in our form room and in the end I think that he got quite annoyed, with <u>almost over half</u> of our class <u>keep having</u> to go back and collect books from our desks. It was even more frightening when he had all of the older pupils in there, they did not look too happy either. Although, at the same time, I had made a whole lot of new friends and I very much loved being at my new school.

In marking this question, examiners were looking for a focus on:
- the ability to write in an appropriate register;
- convincing use of apt style to convey emotion, detail or setting.

Examiner's comments
- The candidate gives a good, detailed, well-organised account of the experience.
- Language is sound and appropriate but could be more **ambitious and flexible**.
- Technical control is sound, with only a few minor errors, except for some mistakes over **sentence punctuation**, which should be rectified for higher grades.

GRADE AWARDED FOR THIS QUESTION: GRADE C

Paper 3F: Media (unseen)

Question 1 *(25 marks for Reading)*

- **Study the advertisement which has been given to you.**
  In what ways does the advertisement try to persuade you that the Sinclair ZETA would be a good buy? Your answer should refer to:
      the type of information given
      the use of language
      the use of illustrations and graphic
      the overall design and layout of the advertisement

Main assessment objective: evaluate how information is presented (including use of presentation, structural and linguistic devices)

Candidate's response
The advert for the new Sinclair Zeta, try's to persuade you that the Sinclair Zeta would be a good buy it gives you a lot of information about the product. It tells you how to use the product 'To use ZETA simply touch the 'on/off' switch on the handle bar'.

It also gives you points on how long it lasts and how fast it can go aswell as giving you information about recharging the battery. The advert uses very good language which often makes you think about your past's with a bike,
"Have you ever cycled up a hill and had to get off and walk?"

This statement makes you look back at the past and makes you wonder if it would be easier if you had the new Sinclair ZETA

"Have you ever wished someone would come up with an igenious invention to take the effort out of pedalling when it gets to much."

Again this statement makes you think about the times when riding a bike has got to much, so it automatically makes you think if I had the new Sinclair Zeta than that wouldn't happen.

It also includes statements that make the Sinclair Zeta seem wonderful "it's a worlds first' 'like most brilliant inventions, Zeta is simplicity itself.'

'ZETA is so well engineered that it works well in all weathers.'

These statement persuade you that the new Sinclair Zeta is too good to be true making it seem like a Dream come true.

85

The use of illustration in this advert is very good_they are in colour so it makes the advert nice to look at. There is one major <u>D</u>rawing <u>P</u>laced <u>N</u>ear the top in the middle of the page_this <u>D</u>rawing shows how the Sinclair Zeta looks after it has been fitted in this <u>D</u>rawing_it also gives you information on the speed, Range and the fact that you don't need any tax, insurance or a licence. This gives us a good idea of what it is going to look like.

There are also small illustrations over the page with points about the Sinclair Zeta. These are giving us details that are in the text. These are reminding us of some of the good points about the Sinclair Zeta which remind us and make us remember the Sinclair Zeta_also the illustrations are in colour so you tend to remember them more.

The general layout of this advertisement is very <u>G</u>ood_it tells you all about the Sinclair Zeta before informing you about the cost. Also the title of the advertisement is in <u>B</u>ig <u>B</u>old writing which attracts you to have a look.

'Take the slog out of cycling'.

This is the title of the advert after reading this really you are persuaded to look at the rest of the advert to see what it is about.

Overall this is a very persuasive advertisement which <u>uses the use</u> of illustration in a very good way.

In marking this question, examiners were looking for a focus on:
- appropriate references to the text;
- attempts to examine the details of the advertisement, to support judgements.

Examiner's comments
- This is detailed response, showing a generally sound grasp of intentions.
- The **erratic control of punctuation affects clarity**.
- Occasional insights push the standard towards C – **these are not consistent enough**, however.
- The response fits D Grade Descriptor: 'Shows generally sound awareness of some persuasive techniques', but in places **this could be more strongly developed**.
  GRADE AWARDED FOR THIS QUESTION: GRADE D

Question 2   (25 marks for Writing)

Range of writing: **analyse, review, comment**

- **A newspaper prints a story criticising the ZETA. Imagine you have used the ZETA. Write a letter to the newspaper giving your views. You should write about whether or not:**
  - **it is reliable**
  - **it is easy to control**
  - **its performance matches the claims in the advertisement**
  - **it is good value for money**
  You may also include any other relevant points.

Main assessment objective: use forms for specific purposes

Candidate's response
Dear Sir/Madam,

I am writing to you about the Sinclair ZETA. After reading the advert two months ago I decided that, being a person that uses bikes everywhere, the ZETA seemed like a brilliant buy.

It would be an end to all of the problems they mentioned in the advert, but to my dismay it wasn't. As reliable as they said the ZETA was 'in all weathers', I'm afraid it just isn't. Although it has made some light relief of my efforts to pedal up a hill or ride into a stiff breeze, I've found that in wet weather the ZETA just doesn't work as well. Rain and muddy, wet tyres just don't work well with the ZETA.

Added to this is the controlling of the ZETA, it simply just isn't as easy as touching an on/off button, this is because sometimes the 'on' button just doesn't seem to work, either this or the ZETA just doesn't work up to its expectations. Another thing that bothers me about the ZETA is how long the battery lasts. Yes_it is easy to change, but once changed it hardly seems to last long. I feel that with full time use the 10 miles put in the advert is a bit of an exaggeration.

Although the ZETA isn't totally useless I feel that it is <u>no where</u> near the value for money I thought it would be when I ordered it. Unless all of the statements made about the ZETA in the advert were absolutely true, I don't feel that the ZETA is worth the £144.95 I <u>payed</u> for it. Considering the amount of work the ZETA does for me, which isn't much_I do not feel totally satisfied and will be asking for my money back. I think that your article which criticised the ZETA was a fair one.

Yours sincerely

In marking this question, examiners were looking for a focus on:
- how effectively the candidate had revealed an understanding of the requirements of the question;
- how effectively the candidate had used the written language to produce a relevant response;
- an appropriate tone and register in the writing.

Examiner's comments
- The range of points is very sound.
- The writing communicates clearly with good register and focus, with only occasional technical errors – sentence punctuation.

GRADE AWARDED FOR THIS QUESTION: GRADE C

Question 3   *(25 marks for Writing)*

Range of writing: **argue**, **persuade**, **instruct**
- **Write an article for a magazine for young people using this title:** *Cycling: the best form of transport for the 21st century?*

Main assessment objective: adapt writing for a range of purposes and audiences

Candidate's response
The world is <u>poluted</u> cars, vans, <u>lorys</u>, buses, motor <u>biks</u>, and more are <u>poluting</u> the world just because people have to travel to work, <u>frends</u> home, school, <u>But</u> while you <u>traviling</u> in a transport which damages the earth the earth is getting weaker every minute because we choose to go in a car <u>wheel</u> why don't you use a more <u>enviromental</u> <u>aproach</u> like cycling. Cycling is enjoyed by billions_some people do it for fun_some people do it to save the <u>enviroment</u> but it is great fun <u>infact</u> more than 80% of the population have got bikes and they use then for <u>differn't</u> thing. Another great way to have fun is to go cycling with your family_not only it is

fun_you get to exercise <u>know</u> think_if you travel by car <u>your</u> damaging the <u>enverment</u> <u>your</u> not getting fitter but if you <u>rid</u> a bike as many people do you will not <u>damag</u> the <u>enviroment</u> you will get fit and it is much cheaper to get instead of a car_so why don't you tell your parents stop using the car and cycle. Remember it's your <u>choose</u> so pick the right one for you and for the world. <u>Infact</u> cycling is so popular <u>amoung</u> all ages and is more popular <u>the</u> 30 years ago so by the year 2000 we <u>predect</u> that more people choose to go and ride a bike not just for you for the earth_because if <u>to</u> much <u>polution</u> is in the world we will all die_so please help and let's make the world a happy ending.

In marking this question, examiners were looking for a focus on the quality of the candidate's writing, irrespective of the particular opinions which are expressed, including:
- ○ an attempt to argue a case and persuade the reader;
- ○ appropriate ideas, facts and arguments;
- ○ awareness of the interests of readers of a magazine for young people.

Examiner's comments
- There is **considerable technical weakness, including punctuation errors** (F criteria).
- The information and argument are reasonably clear and there is some capacity to fit the material to audience and purpose (E descriptors).
- **Accuracy and clarity of expression need closer checking.**
- **Sentences are not always divided correctly.**
  GRADE AWARDED FOR THIS QUESTION: GRADE E (JUST: E/F BORDER)

Paper 4H: Twentieth Century Poetry and Non-Fiction (pre-released material)

Question 1   *(25 marks for Reading)*

- **Look again at the poems 'Half-past Two by U A Fanthorpe (page 19 in Tracks 2) and 'Leaving School' by Hugo Williams (page 20 in *Tracks 2*). What similarities and differences are there in the two poets' treatment of the life of the young child at school?**
  Support your answer closely with examples of the poets' use of language to achieve their effects.

Main assessment objective: develop and sustain interpretations of text.

Candidate's response
'Half-past Two' is about a child's punishment for an unspecified offence, which leaves him alone for a very long period, although because he cannot tell the time he does not know how long. This confusion about time is central. 'Leaving School' is also about a child's helplessness. The child has been sent away to a boarding school, where he is confused by school routines. Both poems therefore focus on what school can be like for a young child.

An important difference is the narrative voice. The first poem uses third person narrative. 'He' is the child and 'She' (with a capital letter) is the teacher. This use of third person narrative makes the poem rather impersonal. However, in 'Leaving School', the poem is written in the first person. We learn much more about the child and his school life, and there is a more developed 'plot'.

The language used in 'Half-past Two' is striking and unusual. The first words, 'Once upon a...', suggest the start of a children's story. The first surprise comes on the next word, 'schooltime', which sounds odd. The use of capital letters makes the reader pause on the words 'Something Very Wrong', repeated a few lines later. The child is trying to come to terms with what he cannot comprehend. The use of the capital for She and Time also suggests that these are important ideas for the child.

The fourth stanza gives more examples of how the child is seeking to understand time. Time deals with what really matters to him, such as the magic of 'timeformykisstime', or 'Grantime'. These compound words help to convey the child into a land of fantasy. Compared with these warm words and magical moments, the dull, plodding sound of monotones in 'half-past two', and the ugly onomatopoeia of 'clockface' and 'click', belong to a much less attractive world.

The child is immersed in the world of the imagination, escaping from time into eternity, 'into ever'. This is shattered by the teacher's frantic movements ('scuttling in') and brisk words: 'you'll be late'. The child is 'slotted' back into the rhythm of the everyday world. But time now becomes threatening: 'nexttime'; 'notimeforthatnowtime'. The event has taught the child an important lesson about time, but there is also a sense of loss. Once the secret language of measuring time is grasped it is no longer possible to experience timelessness in the same way.

Time is central too in 'Leaving School'. First, the young age of the boy is emphasised. We also learn that he has had only a basic education, and is behind the others in reading. At the new school, the most important form of time he had to grasp was the timetable. Events happened in a regular, precise pattern. Failure to grasp this resulted in being in the wrong place or arriving at the wrong time. The headmaster's wife tried to turn mastering the timetable into a game, a game he did not understand. The different times of day posed difficulties, particularly lesson time and bedtime. He missed having a parent to provide warmth and comfort. The only time which the boy liked was 'waiting'.

Fanthorpe exploits the richness of language to emphasise the fantasyland which the child inhabits, while Hugo Williams adopts a deliberately simple style in its choice of vocabulary and sentence structure. The language is quite basic, with little complexity of structure or imagery. The short sentences frequently start with 'I', and present direct pictures of the boy's life. The verbs are also simple and direct, usually the basic past tense of narrative: "had", 'thought', 'found', 'liked', 'forgot'. This simplicity highlights the desperate nature of his plight. At the end, he runs away, or imagines he runs away, from school because he feels he cannot cope.

The poets share the capacity to put the reader inside the mind of the child, and to appreciate how baffling school can be for the young. They both also show the vulnerability of childhood, with its loss of innocence and even of magic.

In marking this question, examiners were looking for a focus on:
- candidates' appreciation of childhood emotions, comparing the poets' handling of the theme;
- the selection of examples of the language from the two poems to illustrate this.

Examiner's comments
- This is a mature response, combining analysis with confident interpretation;
- Comparisons are perceptive and well-argued, with apt use of quotations;
- Command of vocabulary and sentence-structure are of a very high standard.

GRADE AWARDED FOR THIS QUESTION: GRADE A

Question 2 (25 marks for Reading)

- **Look again at the two articles 'Big School, Big Trauma' and 'Starting School' (page 29 in *Tracks 2*). Compare the ways in which the two writers deal with the theme, looking at the style and tone of each.**
  Support your answer by close reference to the language used.

Main assessment objective: read with insight and engagement.

Candidate's response

Both writers deal with the subject of starting secondary school and the problems surrounding it. Although both articles are written about the same subject their attitudes are very different. The similarities and differences can be focused on content, point of view and tone, language, purpose, and the effect the article has on the reader.

'Big School, Big Trauma' is more journalistic, and in the form of a report, or a survey. 'Starting School' is by young boy about to start secondary school, it is autobiographical. The two separate articles have two very different points of view and this <u>effects</u> their tone.

The first article's point of view is that starting school is traumatic and fearful, it focuses on how to tackle 'being a small fish in a very big pond'. The article gives advice to teachers and parents on how to help children cope with the transition: for example, Ted Wragg says that 'it's also very important for Year 6 children to spend a day experiencing a fairly normal if slightly staged secondary school day'.

The second article's point of view is more about the good experiences surrounding this change. The article is more optimistic than 'Big School, Big Trauma'. The autobiographical content creates a more personal and informal tone: 'I've been thinking...'. 'Big School, Big Trauma' is structured and <u>reportive</u>, full of research, 'Starting School' is more unstructured.

The first article is in the third person and triggers discussion: 'What should teachers and parents be doing?' The article triggers memories of how it felt starting school, since Rudduck writes that fifth-formers 'harbour vivid memories of the embarrassment of transition'.

The second article is in the first person and is compared <u>to</u> the apprehensions of fellow pupils. The article leads onto more personal stories instead of factual discussions, and focuses on the fact that the writer hasn't 'got any friends there'.

In conclusion, if these two articles had not been published together, side by side in the same paper, on the same day, their effect on the reader would have greatly differed. The contrast creates interest for the reader, and the effect they have together is powerful.

In marking this question, examiners were looking for a focus on:
  ○ the capacity to evaluate the evidence provided;
  ○ the ability to draw on a thoughtful reading of each to provide apt comparisons;
  ○ good analysis of content and language to develop the response.

Examiner's comments

- The range of points made is very sound, with good, well-chosen vocabulary.
- A **secure analytical framework** is followed, although there needed to be **fuller development**.
- **Comparisons** show a clear sense of the difference between the two passages.

GRADE AWARDED FOR THIS QUESTION: GRADE C

Question 3   (25 marks for Writing)

Range of Writing: **inform, explain, describe**

- **Imagine that you are a young boy or girl who has been sent away from home EITHER to go to a boarding school OR to work as one of the domestic staff in a country house.**
  Write a letter home, informing a member of your family about your life and describing your experiences. You may draw on material you have read in *Tracks 2* **or on your other reading or experience.**

Main assessment objective: use and adapt form for specific purpose.

Candidate's response

My dearest mother,

How are things with you? I'm working my fingers to the bone at the moment doing all sorts of jobs for my master. He's not bad, but he's not soft, he's fair and no one could ask for <u>anymore</u>. Lucky it's not lambing at the moment so I have money for this letter. Everyone is trying to get as much work finished now as they can because if they don't then it'll built_up.

I've got a nice rhythm here but some of the smallest things can affect my daily routine. For example, I get up at 6 but if I haven't done something from the day before I get up and do it at 5.30 instead. I feed the master and all of his family at 6.45 so I have 45 minutes to light the fires and clean the kitchen range. That's my worst job because it means I get dirty and have to go and change before 6.45 and breakfast. I wear the dirty clothes from the day before to clean the range. I, then, put the kettle on, wash the kitchen floor and wait for it to dry. After breakfast I clean up all the utensils.

The master saw in the first week how hard all the housework was when I was just left to do it on my own so he employs Jane, you know, the one whose dad worked down Doris's street as a baker.

Well anyway after all the housework's done Jane and me, we have a rest we do, only <u>til</u> about 12 but it's still a break. At 12 we have to get lunch ready for the master's wife. Jane then leaves me to do the washing and collect the food from the village.

I get on really well with people here but you've just got to keep your head down. I want you and dad to be proud of me.

Anyway I must go now. I'll write to you again soon and I'll try and see you after lambing. Your beloved daughter
Peggy

In marking this question, examiners were looking for:
- ○ the ability to write in the required register for a letter of this kind;
- ○ good awareness of the need to communicate information and to describe and explain clearly.

Examiner's comments

- This is direct and immediate, with good use of detail.
- The candidate is successful in creating an appropriate atmosphere and register.
- Only a few errors of spelling or punctuation.
- The ideas could be developed more fully to give a stronger sense of the girl's life.

GRADE AWARDED FOR THIS QUESTION: GRADE B

Paper 5F: Media (unseen)

Question 1   *(25 marks for Reading)*

- **Study the two leaflets which have been given to you. One was produced by the Whale and Dolphin Conservation Society (WFDCS) and the other by the Royal Society for the Protection of Birds (RSPB). Each leaflet tries to persuade readers to give money to the charity. Compare the persuasive techniques used in the leaflets. You may wish to comment on the following but are free to refer to any other relevant points:**
  - **the ways in which the subject matter is organised and presented**
  - **the use of language**
  - **the design and layout of the leaflets**
  - **reasons why you consider one leaflet to be more accessible than the other.**

Main assessment objective: evaluate how information is presented (including use of presentational, structural and linguistic devices)

Candidate's response

Both the WDCS brochure and the RSPB brochure attempt to attract and persuade the reader into sending money to save the dolphins and birds respectively. Each uses many methods of persuasion, from physical rewards in return to money sent, to emphasising the beauty of the animal.

Both have very appealing covers: the WDCS brochure uses a well-taken photograph of two dolphins rising out of the water simultaneously, attempting to illustrate the 'beauty', 'intelligence' and 'friendliness' of the dolphins, words used to complement the photograph in the brochure itself; the RSPB also uses a very well-taken photograph of a large group of physically beautiful birds, looking grand in mid-flight, to illustrate to the reader the beauty of that which will be supported by the funds. This is a very common, yet persuasive method, used in many brochures and advertisements.

One <u>noteable</u> difference, again on the cover, is that the WDCS brochure uses words as well as pictures to persuade the reader to continue reading the brochure, while the RSPB <u>belives</u> that a more persuasive method is to use less writing, but larger and to the point, simply stating the cause of the charity and the name of the Society, "Help save our BIRDS and wildlife... join the RSPB now." Then in an attempt to attract the attention of people that revel in the chance to receive free goods, states in the top right-hand corner of the brochure, "Free <u>birtable</u>".

Once both brochures are opened it becomes evident that two very different styles are used. In the RSPB brochure, the information given is categorised under five different headings: The first, "The work of the RSPB", is an attempt, not only to state the work of the society but also to make the reader feel guilty, and make him believe that it is his fault that many of these beautiful birds are dying and losing out; the second 'The benefits to you', is again aimed at the audience that needs to benefit <u>himself</u> in order to help others. This is the same audience that the 'free birdtable' was aimed at. This is just a list of benefits, from 'Free access' to nature reserves to "knowledge that you are helping conservation"; this is then followed by the application forms and on the back three pages of the brochure: the RSPB states the membership prices, immediately followed by <u>reasurence</u> that one would receive that 'FREE' birdtable in return; and a list of ways that 'Your support enables us to:'. On the other hand the WDCS uses the brochure to explain the running of the society; to give information on eight different dolphins available for adoption; to tell the reader how unique and exciting this process is; and finally, at the back, the application form.

One method of <u>benefitting</u> the presentation and atmosphere is the use of browns, greens and other colours we <u>asociate</u> with forests, trees and nature.

The WDCS uses a more attractive language, with words such as "thrill", "beautiful", "fascinating" and "wonders". While the RSPB uses language such as "Free", "your benefits", "we need your support", emphasising that this process benefits both us and 'you'.

Altogether I found the WDCS more attractive because I preferred the presentation of it, and the methods they used, in my eyes, were more persuasive to the reader and I was particularly <u>taken in</u> by the use of information on each dolphin.

In marking this question, examiners were looking for:
- ○ a focus on how particular techniques were used to persuade the readers;
- ○ insight into the language and other textual features.

Examiner's comments
- The candidate shows a good understanding of the two leaflets and requirement of the question, but for **an A grade the evaluation could have been a little more convincing**.
- Effective points are made.
- There are **some technical slips which suggested room for more careful checking** – high B.

GRADE AWARDED FOR THIS QUESTION: GRADE B

Question 2   *(25 marks for Writing)*

Range of writing: **analyse**, **review**, **comment**

- **Imagine you are employed to raise money for either the WDCS or the RSPB. Write about three advertising methods which you would use. Explain what you see as the advantages and disadvantages of each of your chosen methods. You may wish to consider any of the following:**
National newspaper advertising, local newspaper advertising, direct mail shots, posters, press releases, leaflets, billboards, or some other form of advertising.

Main assessment objective: use and adapt form for specific purpose

Candidate's response
As an employee of the RSPB, a society which relies heavily on public support, using persuasive advertising would be a very important part of my job. My aim would be to convince as many people as possible, without exhausting the resources of the Society. I would primarily use three methods of advertising; magazine advertising, television advertising, and advertising in national newspapers. Millions of people regularly watch television and read magazines and newspapers.

To use television advertising effectively would require very careful planning. The advertisements would be long enough to be persuasive, yet not too long, resulting in too much expense. The advertisements would have to explain how the RSPB helps to protect birds from disease, pollution and other problems, yet graphic images might not be allowed until after the watershed. Instead I would choose to concentrate more on the good work of the Society than on the plight of birds without public support from the RSPB. Beautiful images of birds flying over stunning scenery would stir up emotions in many people. The advertisements would also have to

93

show the benefits of joining the society. Viewers could see families enjoying days out at RSPB reserves, or reading the free magazines. Any other free offers would be shown, such as the free bird table described in the leaflet. I would have to choose also the times at which the advertisements would be most effective.

The main advantage of this advertising would be that the public would see, without the effort of reading, the advantages of membership of the RSPB. The advertisements would also be seen by a huge number of people. After all, people often don't read advertisements in leaflets yet they rarely switch off the television when they find one advertisement boring. As a free phone number would be given to the viewer as a way to join, he would not be confronted by any time_consuming filling in of forms. The main disadvantage would be the huge expense of producing and then showing the advertisements, which could cost the RSPB a huge sum of money.

The use of national newspaper advertising would be a lot less expensive. The advertisement would also be seen, though not necessarily read, by a huge audience. The advertisement would probably have to be in black and white, so I would concentrate primarily on text rather than photographs or other images. It would be important to use a large text size and to give the reader, as concisely as possible, reasons why he would join the society. It would be good to describe any special offers to encourage the reader to join or to send off for more information. An order form or freephone telephone number would be included. It would also be important to include the logo, which is well known and respected, in a prominent position. This would show the reader that the advertisement is for a well trusted, long established charity.

The newspaper advertising would be less expensive and would reach many people who do not watch television regularly. It would also be easier to produce the advertisement. The main disadvantage would be that a lot of people would inevitably not read or would completely ignore the advertisement. The advertising would therefore have less effect than television advertising.

Advertising in certain popular magazines would be another relatively inexpensive form of advertising. Advertisements could be in full colour and take up a whole page or a double page spread. The magazines would be selected so that readers would be known to like birds, animals or wildlife in general. For example an advertisement in 'National Geographic' would be far more useful than the same advertisement for the RSPB in 'Vogue'.

The magazine could be a good format for large glossy photographs of birds in their natural habitat. Equally, it would be possible to show the suffering of birds in graphic detail. The format would also allow a good amount of large text, so many arguments could be used. The advertisements could also include order forms which the reader could easily cut out. Any offers and the membership pack could be shown with photographs and bright text to be very persuasive. This form of advertising would therefore reach the smallest audience of the three, but would also be likely to convince the highest percentage of that audience to join.

In marking this question, examiners were looking for:
- a clear analysis of three different methods used by fund-raisers;
- evaluative comment on advantages and disadvantages of each;
- clear and precise use of language.

Examiner's comments
- The candidate analyses advantages and disadvantages in a sharply-focused and arresting manner.

- Analysis is 'assured and well-constructed'.
- Overall, the answer meets the descriptors for Grade A*: a pleasure to read for its lucidity and control.

GRADE AWARDED FOR THIS QUESTION: GRADE A*

NB This response captures a fully convincing register, combined with close analysis and comment, evaluating advantages and disadvantages effectively. It has also been checked carefully to ensure accuracy in spelling and punctuation.

Question 3   *(25 marks for Writing)*

Range of writing: **argue**, **persuade**, **instruct**

- **Write a speech for a classroom debate on a topic about which you feel strongly. You could choose a local, national or worldwide issue.**

Main assessment objective: adapt writing for particular purposes and audiences

Candidate's response

Today I am going to talk about the way that the media <u>continally</u> makes people feel that they have to live up to certain visual images_they do this by constantly giving us images of people with perfect bodies. Teenage magazines don't totally exclude people who don't fit in to this image as they do <u>oftern</u> have <u>feature</u> on larger model_but <u>altough</u> they do this it is <u>oftern</u> seen as a <u>once off</u> feature rather than a constant presence in the magazine. By making a big deal about big models they are saying that it's not the norm.

This isn't just a feature of teenage magazines_most <u>womens</u> <u>magazine</u> _constantly have a diet feature making you feel guilty unless on a diet or exercising.

This is part of the reason which makes people feel that they must diet or feel depressed and eat more. There are other examples of the way that the media mistreat people this is a problem that not only <u>affect</u> <u>girl</u> there has been recent _<u>publisity</u> for the fact that 1 in 4 <u>bulimac</u> and <u>anerexic</u> are boys.

I am not saying that all models should be big because again this is giving a single visual image which is the main problem_the lack of differences_and this <u>doen't</u> stand for just size many teenage magazines in particular don't give enough positive images for African and Asian girls_for disabled people and even girls that where glasses_these magazines should include a fair cross section. Some magazines have claimed that this is because aren't enough of these models but if they were to ask for them then the model <u>agenises</u> would be forced to sign the girls.

<u>Unfortunatly</u> I feel the only way we can really change the way that these magazines reflect society is by boycotting them. As all media <u>is</u> <u>primaly</u> based around making money the only way to <u>effect</u> them is where it hurts in the pocket.

And it may seem that one person can't have any <u>affect</u> if every person who felt the same was to do something constructive then it would make a difference.

In marking this question, examiners were looking for:

- ○ answers which showed an understanding of the purpose of the speech and an awareness of audience;
- ○ responses which set out the issues clearly and identified the speaker's particular perspective.

Examiner's comments

- This definitely has some suitable argument and persuasion.
- There are **a number of errors in expression and accuracy of spelling and punctuation**, despite 'some awareness of audience and purpose' – Grade D descriptor; for the higher grades, **the writing would have needed greater clarity and control, and a more varied and subtle vocabulary**.
  GRADE AWARDED FOR THIS QUESTION: GRADE D

Acknowledgements

We are grateful to the following for permission to reproduce copyright material:

Green Flag Group for extract from Barclays car insurance brochure, 1998 **pp. 69–70**.

Help the Aged for 'Adopt a Granny' advertisement, 1998 **p. 61**.

The Independent/Syndication for extract from article by David Lister, 'Disgraceful verse tops poll', *The Independent*, 10.10.96 **p. 32**.

John Johnson (Authors' Agent) Ltd for Jenny Joseph: 'Warning' from *Selected Poems* (Bloodaxe Books, 1992), copyright © Jenny Joseph 1992 **p. 32**.

The Lancet Ltd for extracts from interview with Jenny Joseph, *The Lancet*, vol 354, supplement 3, 6.11.99, copyright © The Lancet Ltd, 1999 **p. 33**.

Leeds Castle Enterprises Ltd for day visitor leaflet, 1998 **pp. 65–67**.

News International Syndication for article by Neil Syson, 'Cyber pets will escape quarantine', *The Sun*, 21.9.98, copyright © News International Newspapers Ltd, 1998 **p. 59**.

Oxfam Publishing, 274 Banbury Road, Oxford OX2 7DZ for Oxfam's Fast and competition leaflet, 'You'd be a mug to miss out...', Oxfam GB 1998 **p. 62**.

Peterloo Poets for U A Fanthorpe: 'Half-past Two' and 'Old Man, Old Man' from *A Watching Brief* (1987); and 'You Will be Hearing From Us Shortly' and 'Reports' from *Standing To* (1982); all poems copyright © U A Fanthorpe **p. 14, 16, 21, 30**.

Vernon Scannell for 'Hide and Seek' from his *Collected Poems* 1950-1993 (Robson Books, 1993) **p. 24**.

Wole Soyinka, via Morton L Leavy, Attorney, on behalf of the author for Wole Soyinka: 'Telephone Conversation' from *A Selection of African Poetry* edited by K E Senanu and T Vincent (Longman, 1976) **p. 28**.

Transworld Publishers, a division of the Random House Group Ltd for extract from *Notes from a Small Island* by Bill Bryson (Black Swan, 1995), copyright © Bill Bryson 1995. All rights reserved **pp. 46–47**.

Hugo Williams for 'Leaving School' from *Selected Poems* (OUP, 1989), copyright © Hugo Williams 1989 **p. 26**.

PHOTOGRAPHS:

Peterloo Poets, photo of UA Fanthorpe by RV Bailey **p.14**; Vernon Scannell, photo by Alan Benson **p. 24**; Hugo Williams **p. 26**; Wole Soyinka, courtesy of Methuen Publishing Ltd **p. 28**; Topham Picturepoint **pp. 44, 48**.

Cover pictures: Maya Angelou, courtesy of Virago; Robert Browning, Aldridge Archive; Carol Ann Duffy by Chris McKee, courtesy of Anvil Press; Tony Harrison (Gordon Dickerson).